In *100 Poems to Lift Your Spirits,* You'll Find . . .

Joy in nature . . .

> "There is a pleasure in the pathless woods,
> There is a rapture on the lonely shore,
> There is society, where none intrudes,
> By the deep sea, and music in its roar."
>
> —*from "There Is a Pleasure in the Pathless Woods" by Lord Byron*

Fun in nonsense and wordplay . . .

> "Beautiful Soup, so rich and green,
> Waiting in a hot tureen!
> Who for such dainties would not stoop?
> Soup of the evening, beautiful Soup!"
>
> —*from "Beautiful Soup" by Lewi~~s C~~*

Comfort in words of th~~e~~

> "All things bright and be
> All creatures great and s~~i~~
> All things wise and wonderful,
> The Lord God made them all."
>
> —*from "Maker of Heaven and Earth" by Cecil Frances Alexander*

Harmony in our universal human connections . . .

> "There are pioneer souls that blaze the paths
> Where highways never ran—
> But let me live by the side of the road
> And be a friend to man."
>
> —*from "The House by the Side of the Road" by Sam Walter Foss*

Also Edited by Leslie Pockell

The 100 Best Poems of All Time

The 100 Best Love Poems of All Time

The 13 Best Horror Stories of All Time

Everything I've Learned

The 101 Greatest Business Principles of All Time

The 100 Greatest Sales Tips of All Time

The 100 Greatest Leadership Principles of All Time

100
POEMS
TO LIFT YOUR
SPIRITS

Edited by

Leslie Pockell

with Celia Johnson

GC

GRAND CENTRAL
PUBLISHING

NEW YORK   BOSTON

Some poems have been reprinted by permission, which the editors and publisher gratefully acknowledge in detail in the Acknowledgments section of this book, beginning on page 205.

Grand Central Publishing
Hachette Book Group USA
237 Park Avenue
New York, NY 10017

Visit our Web site at www.HachetteBookGroupUSA.com.

Book design and text composition by Ralph Fowler

Printed in the United States of America

First Edition: March 2008
10 9 8 7 6 5 4 3 2 1

Grand Central Publishing is a division of Hachette Book Group USA, Inc.
The Grand Central Publishing name and logo is a trademark of Hachette Book Group USA, Inc.

Library of Congress Cataloging-in-Publication Data

100 poems to lift your spirits / edited by Leslie Pockell with Celia Johnson. — 1st ed.
   p.   cm.
Includes index.
ISBN-13: 978-0-446-17795-5
ISBN-10: 0-446-17795-4
   1. English poetry.   2. American poetry.   I. Pockell, Leslie.   II. Johnson, Celia.   III. Title: One hundred poems to lift your spirits.
PR1175.A137175   2008
821.008—dc22   2007037698

CONTENTS

NONSENSE

SPIRITUALITY

THE HUMAN CONNECTION

INTRODUCTION

Everybody gets the blues sometimes. It's a natural part of life, when things are not going well or often for no special reason at all. Nobody really understands why at times you just don't feel good about yourself or the world at large, and pharmaceutical firms and liquor stores have made a great deal of money out of people's natural urge to find a pill or a drink to make them feel better instantly. This book offers the promise of much less expensive and longer-lasting relief from such symptoms, and has the side benefit of not requiring a prescription or a notice warning the reader not to operate heavy machinery after using it!

We've divided the hundred poems contained here into four sections, each with a different approach to improving your mood. First comes a section of poems about **Nature**, because a sense of kinship and harmony with the natural world has an almost inherently tonic effect. Next is a section of **Nonsense** poems, because nothing makes us feel better than the simple act of laughter. Following that is a section of **Spiritual** poems, which connect us to a more transcendent sense of existence, in which our experiences are part of a larger universe. Finally comes **The Human Connection**, which contains poems linking us to others around us whose cares and joys we share.

The result of all this, we hope, is that you the reader will lose yourself amid the poetry collected here—some of it the highest literature, some more down-to-earth, but calculated to relieve your worries all the same—while finding images, thoughts, and expressions that resonate with your own hopes, wishes, and concerns. And we firmly believe that, in the process of gaining sustenance and emotional support from the contents of this book, you will find your spirits lifted, your mood improved, and your cares dispersed.

We recommend you keep this book by your bedside or close at hand, so that you can administer its healing words whenever you feel the need. Enjoy the poems and the world they describe.

—Leslie Pockell
Celia Johnson
New York City, 2008

NATURE

William Wordsworth wrote about nature as though it were his religion (which perhaps it was). In these two poems he communicates with almost mystical fervor the connection between human beings and the natural world that he felt ennobles our lives and makes them worth living. (For a comic transformation of the second poem, turn to p. 49 for the wildly nonsensical "I Wandered Lonely as a Clod.")

THE RAINBOW

William Wordsworth
(1770–1850)

My heart leaps up when I behold
A rainbow in the sky:
So was it when my life began;
So is it now I am a man;
So be it when I shall grow old,
     Or let me die!
The Child is father of the Man;
And I could wish my days to be
Bound each to each by natural piety.

DAFFODILS

William Wordsworth

(1770–1850)

I wander'd lonely as a cloud
    That floats on high o'er vales and hills,
When all at once I saw a crowd,
    A host, of golden daffodils;
Beside the lake, beneath the trees,
Fluttering and dancing in the breeze.

Continuous as the stars that shine
    And twinkle on the Milky Way,
They stretched in never-ending line
    Along the margin of a bay:
Ten thousand saw I at a glance,
Tossing their heads in sprightly dance.

The waves beside them danced; but they
    Out-did the sparkling waves in glee:
A poet could not but be gay,
    In such a jocund company:
I gazed—and gazed—but little thought
What wealth the show to me had brought:

For oft, when on my couch I lie
    In vacant or in pensive mood,
They flash upon that inward eye
    Which is the bliss of solitude;
And then my heart with pleasure fills,
And dances with the daffodils.

Lord Byron (George Gordon Byron) was perhaps the most roman-
tic (in all senses of the word) of the poets of the English Romantic
movement. Much of his poetry is satirical or melodramatic, but
here his passionate identification with the natural world around
him is as powerful as Wordsworth's.

THERE IS A PLEASURE IN THE PATHLESS WOODS

George Gordon, Lord Byron
(1788–1824)

There is a pleasure in the pathless woods,
There is a rapture on the lonely shore,
There is society, where none intrudes,
By the deep Sea, and music in its roar:
I love not Man the less, but Nature more,
From these our interviews, in which I steal
From all I may be, or have been before,
To mingle with the Universe, and feel
What I can ne'er express, yet cannot all conceal.

Percy Shelley led a brief, turbulent, but dazzlingly productive life, much of it concerned with politics, philosophy, and the inspirational role of poets, whom he famously described as "the unacknowledged legislators of the world." In this passionate tribute he celebrates the brilliant, thoughtless creativity of nature.

TO A SKYLARK

Percy Bysshe Shelley
(1792–1822)

Hail to thee, blithe spirit!
   Bird thou never wert,—
That from Heaven or near it
   Pourest thy full heart
In profuse strains of unpremeditated art.

Higher still and higher
   From the earth thou springest,
Like a cloud of fire;
   The blue deep thou wingest,
And singing still dost soar, and soaring ever singest.

In the golden light'ning
   Of the sunken sun
O'er which clouds are bright'ning,
   Thou dost float and run,
Like an unbodied joy whose race is just begun.

The pale purple even
    Melts around thy flight;
Like a star of heaven
    In the broad daylight
Thou art unseen, but yet I hear thy shrill delight—

Keen as are the arrows
    Of that silver sphere,
Whose intense lamp narrows
    In the white dawn clear,
Until we hardly see, we feel that it is there.

All the earth and air
    With thy voice is loud,
As, when night is bare,
    From one lonely cloud
The moon rains out her beams, and heaven is overflow'd.

What thou art we know not;
    What is most like thee?
From rainbow clouds there flow not
    Drops so bright to see,
As from thy presence showers a rain of melody:—

Like a poet hidden
    In the light of thought,
Singing hymns unbidden,
    Till the world is wrought
To sympathy with hopes and fears it heeded not:

Like a high-born maiden
    In a palace tower,
Soothing her love-laden
    Soul in secret hour
With music sweet as love, which overflows her bower:

Like a glow-worm golden
    In a dell of dew,
Scattering unbeholden
    Its aerial hue
Among the flowers and grass, which screen it from the view:

Like a rose embower'd
    In its own green leaves,
By warm winds deflower'd,
    Till the scent it gives
Makes faint with too much sweet these heavy-wingèd thieves.

Sound of vernal showers
    On the twinkling grass,
Rain-awaken'd flowers—
    All that ever was
Joyous, and clear, and fresh—thy music doth surpass.

Teach us, sprite or bird,
    What sweet thoughts are thine:
I have never heard
    Praise of love or wine
That panted forth a flood of rapture so divine.

Chorus hymeneal,
  Or triumphal chant
Match'd with thine, would be all
  But an empty vaunt—
A thing wherein we feel there is some hidden want.

What objects are the fountains
  Of thy happy strain?
What fields, or waves, or mountains?
  What shapes of sky or plain?
What love of thine own kind? what ignorance of pain?

With thy clear keen joyance
  Languor cannot be:
Shadow of annoyance
  Never came near thee:
Thou lovest, but ne'er knew love's sad satiety.

Waking or asleep,
  Thou of death must deem
Things more true and deep
  Than we mortals dream,
Or how could thy notes flow in such a crystal stream?

We look before and after,
  And pine for what is not:
Our sincerest laughter
  With some pain is fraught;
Our sweetest songs are those that tell of saddest thought.

Yet, if we could scorn
    Hate, and pride, and fear,
If we were things born
    Not to shed a tear,
I know not how thy joy we ever should come near.

Better than all measures
    Of delightful sound,
Better than all treasures
    That in books are found,
Thy skill to poet were, thou scorner of the ground!

Teach me half the gladness
    That thy brain must know;
Such harmonious madness
    From my lips would flow,
The world should listen then, as I am listening now!

The first of these poems, published not long before the poet's death, evokes no sense of the imminence of winter and the approach of year's end. Rather it celebrates both the fullness of the harvest, and the almost riotous abundance of life at this time of fruition. The second poem is a lyrical and heartbreakingly eloquent celebration of the rhythm of the seasons and the natural continuity of existence.

TO AUTUMN

John Keats

(1795–1821)

Season of mists and mellow fruitfulness!
　　Close bosom-friend of the maturing sun;
Conspiring with him how to load and bless
　　With fruit the vines that round the thatch-eves run;
To bend with apples the moss'd cottage-trees,
　　And fill all fruit with ripeness to the core;
　　　　To swell the gourd, and plump the hazel shells
　　With a sweet kernel; to set budding more,
And still more, later flowers for the bees,
Until they think warm days will never cease,
　　For Summer has o'er-brimm'd their clammy cells.

Who hath not seen thee oft amid thy store?
　　Sometimes whoever seeks abroad may find
Thee sitting careless on a granary floor,
　　Thy hair soft-lifted by the winnowing wind;

Or on a half-reap'd furrow sound asleep,
    Drows'd with the fume of poppies, while thy hook
        Spares the next swath and all its twined flowers:
And sometimes like a gleaner thou dost keep
    Steady thy laden head across a brook;
    Or by a cyder-press, with patient look,
        Thou watchest the last oozings hours by hours.

Where are the songs of Spring? Ay, where are they?
    Think not of them, thou hast thy music too,—
While barrèd clouds bloom the soft-dying day,
    And touch the stubble-plains with rosy hue;
Then in a wailful choir the small gnats mourn
    Among the river sallows, borne aloft
        Or sinking as the light wind lives or dies;
And full-grown lambs loud bleat from hilly bourn;
    Hedge-crickets sing; and now with treble soft
    The red breast whistles from a garden-croft;
        And gathering swallows twitter in the skies.

ON THE GRASSHOPPER
AND CRICKET

John Keats

(1795–1821)

The poetry of earth is never dead;
When all the birds are faint with the hot sun,
And hide in cooling trees, a voice will run
From hedge to hedge about the new-mown mead;
That is the grasshopper's—he takes the lead
In summer luxury,—he has never done
With his delights, for when tired out with fun
He rests at ease beneath some pleasant weed.
The poetry of earth is ceasing never:
On a lone winter evening, when the frost
Has wrought a silence, from the stove there shrills
The cricket's song, in warmth increasing ever,
And seems to one in drowsiness half lost,
The grasshopper's among some grassy hills.

Anne Brontë, less known than her two sisters, was nonetheless a gifted and sensitive creative artist. While in "To Autumn" Keats celebrates the life-affirming bounty of autumn, in this poem Brontë is uplifted by the wild beauty of a gusty winter's day.

LINES COMPOSED IN A WOOD ON A WINDY DAY

Anne Brontë

(1820–1849)

My soul is awakened, my spirit is soaring
And carried aloft on the wings of the breeze;
For above and around me the wild wind is roaring,
Arousing to rapture the earth and the seas.

The long withered grass in the sunshine is glancing,
The bare trees are tossing their branches on high;
The dead leaves beneath them are merrily dancing,
The white clouds are scudding across the blue sky

I wish I could see how the ocean is lashing
The foam of its billows to whirlwinds of spray;
I wish I could see how its proud waves are dashing,
And hear the wild roar of their thunder to-day!

This classic reflection on the joys of solitude describes a garden not far short of an Edenic paradise, yet the pleasures taken by the poet within the garden are clearly meant to evoke a sense of the erotic. Taken together these elements convert a transfiguring mystical experience into one almost carnal, despite the deceptively mild final stanza. This poem is followed by a contrasting one in which the poet finds a metaphysical connection between a drop of dew and the human soul.

THOUGHTS IN A GARDEN

Andrew Marvell

(1621–1678)

How vainly men themselves amaze
To win the palm, the oak, or bays,
And their uncessant labours see
Crown'd from some single herb or tree,
Whose short and narrow-vergèd shade
Does prudently their toils upbraid;
While all the flowers and trees do close
To weave the garlands of repose!

Fair Quiet, have I found thee here,
And Innocence thy sister dear?
Mistaken long, I sought you then
In busy companies of men:
Your sacred plants, if here below,
Only among the plants will grow:
Society is all but rude
To this delicious solitude.

No white nor red was ever seen
So amorous as this lovely green.
Fond lovers, cruel as their flame,
Cut in these trees their mistress' name:
Little, alas! they know or heed
How far these beauties hers exceed!
Fair trees! wheres'e'er your barks I wound,
No name shall but your own be found.

When we have run our passions' heat,
Love hither makes his best retreat:
The gods, that mortal beauty chase,
Still in a tree did end their race;
Apollo hunted Daphne so
Only that she might laurel grow;
And Pan did after Syrinx speed
Not as a nymph, but for a reed.

What wondrous life in this I lead!
Ripe apples drop about my head;
The luscious clusters of the vine
Upon my mouth do crush their wine;
The nectarine and curious peach
Into my hands themselves do reach;
Stumbling on melons, as I pass,
Ensnared with flowers, I fall on grass.

Meanwhile the mind from pleasure less
Withdraws into its happiness;
The mind, that ocean where each kind
Does straight its own resemblance find;
Yet it creates, transcending these,

Far other worlds, and other seas;
Annihilating all that's made
To a green thought in a green shade.

Here at the fountain's sliding foot,
Or at some fruit-tree's mossy root,
Casting the body's vest aside,
My soul into the boughs does glide;
There, like a bird, it sits and sings,
Then whets and combs its silver wings,
And, till prepared for longer flight,
Waves in its plumes the various light.

Such was that happy Garden-state
While man there walk'd without a mate:
After a place so pure and sweet,
What other help could yet be meet!
But 'twas beyond a mortal's share
To wander solitary there:
Two paradises 'twere in one,
To live in Paradise alone.

How well the skilful gard'ner drew
Of flowers and herbs this dial new!
Where, from above, the milder sun
Does through a fragrant zodiac run:
And, as it works, th' industrious bee
Computes its time as well as we.
How could such sweet and wholesome hours
Be reckon'd, but with herbs and flowers!

ON A DROP OF DEW

Andrew Marvell

(1621–1678)

See how the orient dew
Shed from the bosom of the Morn
Into the blowing roses,
Yet careless of its mansion new;
For the clear region where 'twas born,
Round in its self incloses:
And in its little globe's extent
Frames, as it can, its native element.
How it the purple flow'r does slight,
Scarce touching where it lies,
But gazing back upon the skies,
Shines with a mournful light,
Like its own tear,
Because so long divided from the sphere.
Restless it rolls and unsecure,
Trembling lest it grow impure;
Till the warm sun pity its pain,
And to the skies exhale it back again.
So the soul, that drop, that ray
Of the clear fountain of eternal day,
Could it within the human flow'r be seen,
Rememb'ring still its former height,
Shuns the sweet leaves and blossoms green,
And, recollecting its own light,
Does in its pure and circling thoughts express
The greater heaven in an heaven less.

In how coy a figure wound,
Every way it turns away;
(So the world excluding round)
Yet receiving in the day.
Dark beneath, but bright above;
Here disdaining, there in love.
How loose and easy hence to go;
How girt and ready to ascend;
Moving but on a point below,
It all about does upwards bend.
Such did the manna's sacred dew distil;
White and intire, though congeal'd and chill.
Congeal'd on Earth: but does, dissolving, run
Into the glories of th' Almighty Sun.

Emerson, among his other accomplishments, was a poet of Nature, which he regarded as an expression of the divine. The first poem here, however, bears little philosophical weight, and with its cheerful couplets depicts an enjoyable journey accompanying that familiar garden companion we today call the bumble bee. In the second, the poet reflects on a wildflower seldom seen by human eyes, but which nonetheless has as much reason to exist as we all do.

THE HUMBLE BEE

Ralph Waldo Emerson
(1803–1882)

Burly, dozing humble-bee,
Where thou art is clime for me.
Let them sail for Porto Rique,
Far-off heats through seas to seek;
I will follow thee alone,
Thou animated torrid-zone!
Zigzag steerer, desert cheerer,
Let me chase thy waving lines;
Keep me nearer, me thy hearer,
Singing over shrubs and vines.

Insect lover of the sun,
Joy of thy dominion!
Sailor of the atmosphere;
Swimmer through the waves of air;
Voyager of light and noon;

Epicurean of June;
Wait, I prithee, till I come
Within earshot of thy hum,—
All without is martyrdom.

When the south wind, in May days,
With a net of shining haze
Silvers the horizon wall,
And with softness touching all,
Tints the human countenance
With a color of romance,
And infusing subtle heats,
Turns the sod to violets,
Thou, in sunny solitudes,
Rover of the underwoods,
The green silence dost displace
With thy mellow, breezy bass.

Hot midsummer's petted crone,
Sweet to me thy drowsy tone
Tells of countless sunny hours,
Long days, and solid banks of flowers;
Of gulfs of sweetness without bound
In Indian wildernesses found;
Of Syrian peace, immortal leisure,
Firmest cheer, and bird-like pleasure.

Aught unsavory or unclean
Hath my insect never seen;
But violets and bilberry bells,
Maple-sap and daffodels,
Grass with green flag half-mast high,

Succory to match the sky,
Columbine with horn of honey,
Scented fern, and agrimony,
Clover, catchfly, adder's-tongue
And brier-roses, dwelt among;
All beside was unknown waste,
All was picture as he passed.

Wiser far than human seer,
Yellow-breeched philosopher!
Seeing only what is fair,
Sipping only what is sweet,
Thou dost mock at fate and care,
Leave the chaff, and take the wheat.
When the fierce northwestern blast
Cools sea and land so far and fast,
Thou already slumberest deep;
Woe and want thou canst outsleep;
Want and woe, which torture us,
Thy sleep makes ridiculous.

RHODORA

Ralph Waldo Emerson
(1803–1882)

On being asked, whence is the flower.
In May, when sea-winds pierced our solitudes,
I found the fresh Rhodora in the woods,
Spreading its leafless blooms in a damp nook,
To please the desert and the sluggish brook.
The purple petals fallen in the pool
Made the black water with their beauty gay;
Here might the red-bird come his plumes to cool,
And court the flower that cheapens his array.
Rhodora! if the sages ask thee why
This charm is wasted on the earth and sky,
Tell them, dear, that, if eyes were made for seeing,
Then beauty is its own excuse for Being;
Why thou wert there, O rival of the rose!
I never thought to ask; I never knew;
But in my simple ignorance suppose
The self-same power that brought me there, brought you.

Around 2400 years ago, Euclid set forth principles of geometry that are still followed today, but in the poet's lovely conceit, measuring the universe is less important than appreciating its beauty. The second poem here by Lindsay projects a reverie of vivid and fantastic images onto the surface of the moon with such clarity that it almost seems they should be visible to the naked eye.

EUCLID

Vachel Lindsay
(1879–1931)

Old Euclid drew a circle
On a sand-beach long ago.
He bounded and enclosed it
With angles thus and so.
His set of solemn greybeards
Nodded and argued much
Of arc and circumference,
Diameter and such.
A silent child stood by them
From morning until noon
Because they drew such charming
Round pictures of the moon.

DRYING THEIR WINGS

Vachel Lindsay

(1879–1931)

(What the Carpenter Said)

The moon's a cottage with a door.
Some folks can see it plain.
Look, you may catch a glint of light,
A sparkle through the pane,
Showing the place is brighter still
Within, though bright without.
There, at a cosy open fire
Strange babes are grouped about.
The children of the wind and tide—
The urchins of the sky,
Drying their wings from storms and things
So they again can fly.

Andrew Marvell found the human soul within a drop of dew (p. 18), but here Walt Whitman finds that a spider endlessly seeking to anchor itself with its silk evokes the soul's yearning to connect itself to the universe. The second poem's tribute to the elemental beauty of nature recalls Vachel Lindsay's poem "Euclid" (p. 24).

A NOISELESS, PATIENT SPIDER

Walt Whitman
(1819–1892)

A noiseless, patient spider,
I mark'd, where, on a little promontory, it stood, isolated;
Mark'd how, to explore the vacant, vast surrounding,
It launch'd forth filament, filament, filament, out of itself;
Ever unreeling them—ever tirelessly speeding them.

And you, O my Soul, where you stand,
Surrounded, surrounded, in measureless oceans of space,
Ceaselessly musing, venturing, throwing,—seeking the
    spheres, to connect them;
Till the bridge you will need, be form'd—till the ductile
    anchor hold;
Till the gossamer thread you fling, catch somewhere, O
    my Soul.

WHEN I HEARD THE LEARN'D ASTRONOMER

Walt Whitman

(1819–1892)

When I heard the learn'd astronomer;
When the proofs, the figures, were ranged in columns
    before me;
When I was shown the charts and the diagrams, to add,
    divide, and measure them;
When I, sitting, heard the astronomer, where he lectured
    with much applause in the lecture-room,
How soon, unaccountable, I became tired and sick;
Till rising and gliding out, I wander'd off by myself,
In the mystical moist night-air, and from time to time,
Look'd up in perfect silence at the stars.

This first optimistic poem is from a larger work by Browning, "Pippa Passes," which describes the effect of a pure, high-spirited young girl on the darker world through which she wanders, untouched by its miseries. "Among the Rocks," which follows the first poem, portrays the earth in autumn as a smiling old man, well worth our love.

THE YEAR'S AT THE SPRING

Robert Browning
(1812–1889)

The year's at the spring,
And day's at the morn;
Morning's at seven;
The hill-side's dew-pearled;
The lark's on the wing;
The snail's on the thorn;
God's in his Heaven—
All's right with the world!

AMONG THE ROCKS

Robert Browning

(1812–1889)

Oh, good gigantic smile o' the brown old earth,
This autumn morning! How he sets his bones
To bask i' the sun, and thrusts out knees and feet
For the ripple to run over in its mirth;
Listening the while, where on the heap of stones
The white breast of the sea-lark twitters sweet.
That is the doctrine, simple, ancient, true;
Such is life's trial, as old earth smiles and knows.
If you loved only what were worth your love,
Love were clear gain, and wholly well for you:
Make the low nature better by your throes!
Give earth yourself, go up for gain above!

Yeats was a great exponent of Irish folklore, but the images of these two poems transcend their Gaelic elements and articulate universal themes of peaceful solitude and the almost sensual call of the natural world. Andrew Marvell's "Thoughts in a Garden" (p. 15) expresses similar sentiments in a more elaborate form.

THE SONG OF WANDERING AENGUS

William Butler Yeats
(1865–1939)

I went out to the hazel wood,
Because a fire was in my head,
And cut and peeled a hazel wand,
And hooked a berry to a thread;
And when white moths were on the wing,
And moth-like stars were flickering out,
I dropped the berry in a stream
And caught a little silver trout.

When I had laid it on the floor
I went to blow the fire a-flame,
But something rustled on the floor,
And someone called me by my name:
It had become a glimmering girl
With apple blossom in her hair
Who called me by my name and ran
And faded through the brightening air.

Though I am old with wandering
Through hollow lands and hilly lands,
I will find out where she has gone,
And kiss her lips and take her hands;
And walk among long dappled grass,
And pluck till time and times are done,
The silver apples of the moon,
The golden apples of the sun.

THE LAKE ISLE OF INNISFREE

William Butler Yeats

(1865–1939)

I will arise and go now, and go to Innisfree,
And a small cabin build there, of clay and wattles made:
Nine bean-rows will I have there, a hive for the honey-bee,
And live alone in the bee-loud glade.

And I shall have some peace there, for peace comes
    dropping slow,
Dropping from the veils of the morning to where the
    cricket sings;
There midnight's all a glimmer, and noon a purple glow,
And evening full of the linnet's wings.

I will arise and go now, for always night and day
I hear lake water lapping with low sounds by the shore;
While I stand on the roadway, or on the pavements grey,
I hear it in the deep heart's core.

Really, every new day offers its own opportunity for another be-ginning, and this optimistic poem celebrates that fact with every-day imagery to delight all the senses.

DAWN REVISITED

Rita Dove

(1952–)

Imagine you wake up
with a second chance: The blue jay
hawks his pretty wares
and the oak still stands, spreading
glorious shade. If you don't look back,

the future never happens.
How good to rise in sunlight,
in the prodigal smell of biscuits—
eggs and sausage on the grill.
The whole sky is yours

to write on, blown open
to a blank page. Come on,
shake a leg! You'll never know
who's down there, frying those eggs,
if you don't get up and see.

The pharaoh Amenhotep took on the name Akhnaten in homage to the sun god, Aten, and he and his people worshipped only this god throughout his reign. This beautiful prayer is an exultant hymn to the lifegiving power of nature.

POEM IN PRAISE OF THE SUN

Attributed to the Pharaoh Akhnaten
(Reigned c. 1352–1336 B.C.E.)

You arise beauteous in the horizon of the heavens
Oh living Aten the beginning of life.
When you shine forth in the Eastern horizon you fill every
    land with your beauty.
You are so beautiful: you are great; gleaming and high over
    every land.
Your rays embrace the lands and all you have created;
You are Re and reach out to all your creations, and hold
    them for your beloved Son.
You are afar, but your rays touch the earth;
Men see you, but know not your ways.

When you set in the Western horizon of the sky
The earth lies in darkness as in death.
People sleep in their rooms, their heads veiled, and
no eye beholds another.
If all their possessions were stolen
They would know it not.
Every lion leaves its lair;

All snakes bite;
Darkness covers all.
The world is silent
For the creator rests in his horizon.

When you rise from the horizon the earth grows bright;
You shine as the Aten in the sky and drive away the
    darkness;
When your rays gleam forth, the whole of Egypt is festive.
People wake and stand on their feet
For you have lifted them up.
They wash their limbs and take up their clothes and dress;
They raise their arms to you in adoration.

Then the whole of the land does its work;
All cattle enjoy their pastures,
Trees and plants grow green,
Birds fly up from their nests
And raise their wings in praise of your spirit.
Goats frisk on their feet,
And all fluttering and flying things come alive
Because you shine on them.
Boats sail up and downstream,
All ways are opened because you have appeared.
The fish in the river leap up to you
Your rays are in the deep of the sea.

You make the seed grow in women, make fluid into
    mankind;
You give life to the son in his mother's womb
Soothing him so he does not cry
Oh nurse within the womb.

You give the breath of life to all your creations
From the day they are born.
You open their mouths and give them sustenance.
To the chick that cries while still in the egg
You give breath in the shell to let him live,
And make the time for him to break the shell
And come out of the egg at the moment for him to chirp
And patter on his two feet.

How manifold are your works: they are hidden from our
    sight
Oh unique god, no other is like you.
You made the earth after your own heart
When you were alone. All men, herds
And flocks, all on the earth that goes on its feet;
and all that is in the sky and flies with its wings.
The land of Egypt, the foreign lands of Syria and Nubia
    too—
You put every man in his place and fulfill his needs;
Each one with his sustenance and the days of his life
    counted,
Their language is different,
And they look different;
Their complexions are different,
For you have distinguished the nations.
You make the seasons to bring into being all your creatures;
Winter to cool them,
And the heat of summer to come from you.
You have made the sky afar off
So when you rise you can see all you have made.
You alone rise in the form of the living Aten

Shining afar, yet close at hand.
You make millions of forms out of you alone,
Towns and villages, fields, roads and river.
All eyes see you before them
For you are the Aten of the day, over all the earth.
You are in my heart and none other knows thee
But your son "Akhenaten";
You have given him understanding of your designs and
  your strength.

The world is in your hands, as you have made it.
When you have risen, they live,
and when you set, they die,
for you are a lifetime yourself;
men live in you.
Eyes look on perfection until you set.
All work is laid aside when you set on the right hand.
When you rise again, you make every arm stir for the king,
  and
haste is in every limb, since you have founded the earth.
You raise them for your son who came forth from your
  body,
the king of Upper and Lower Egypt, who lives from order,
Akhenaten, and the great royal consort, Nefertiti.

John Masefield spent his early years as a seaman on a sailing ship, and throughout his long life and literary career (he became poet laureate of England), he retained his love of the freedom and wildness of those distant days.

SEA FEVER

John Masefield
(1878–1967)

I must down to the seas again, to the lonely sea and the sky,
And all I ask is a tall ship and a star to steer her by,
And the wheel's kick and the wind's song and the white
    sail's shaking,
And a grey mist on the sea's face, and a grey dawn breaking.

I must down to the seas again, for the call of the running
    tide
Is a wild call and a clear call that may not be denied;
And all I ask is a windy day with the white clouds flying,
And the flung spray and the blown spume, and the sea-gulls
    crying.

I must down to the seas again, to the vagrant gypsy life,
To the gull's way and the whale's way where the wind's like a
    whetted knife;
And all I ask is a merry yarn from a laughing fellow-rover
And quiet sleep and a sweet dream when the long trick's
    over.

Robert Frost was an ardent naturalist, who worshipped the New England landscape where he spent most of his life. In the following poems, the simplest acts of nature incite feelings of euphoria to be treasured and revered.

UNHARVESTED

Robert Frost
(1874–1963)

A scent of ripeness from over a wall.
And come to leave the routine road
And look for what had made me stall,
There sure enough was an apple tree
That had eased itself of its summer load,
And of all but its trivial foliage free,
Now breathed as light as a lady's fan.
For there had been an apple fall
As complete as the apple had given man.
The ground was one circle of solid red.

May something go always unharvested!
May much stay out of our stated plan,
Apples or something forgotten and left,
So smelling their sweetness would be no theft.

ROSE POGONIAS

Robert Frost

(1874–1963)

A saturated meadow,
Sun-shaped and jewel-small,
A circle scarcely wider
Than the trees around were tall;
Where winds were quite excluded,
And the air was stifling sweet
With the breath of many flowers—
A temple of the heat.

There we bowed us in the burning,
As the sun's right worship is,
To pick where none could miss them
A thousand orchises;
For though the grass was scattered,
Yet every second spear
Seemed tipped with wings of color
That tinged the atmosphere.

We raised a simple prayer
Before we left the spot,
That in the general mowing
That place might be forgot;
Or if not all so favored,
Obtain such grace of hours
That none should mow the grass there
While so confused with flowers.

The poetry of E. E. Cummings is notable for its typographical in-genuity almost as much as for its language and sentiments; to-gether they usually form a harmonious union of form and content. The first poem here graphically reproduces the idea of children wandering through a field of flowers. The second is more tradi-tional in its type design, but similarly sensitive to the awakening of a child to the essence of the natural world.

TUMBLING-HAIR

E. E. Cummings
(1894–1962)

Tumbling-hair
                picker of buttercups
                              violets
dandelions
And the big bullying daisies
                    through the field wonderful
with eyes a little sorry
Another comes
          also picking flowers

WHO ARE YOU,LITTLE I

E. E. Cummings

(1894–1962)

(five or six years old)
peering from some high

window;at the gold

of November sunset

(and feeling:that if day
has to become night

this is a beautiful way)

Nature often seems distant and removed from our lives, a phe-
nomenon to be appreciated only from afar. However, the following
poems indicate that human beings are, in fact, natural wonders,
even though we may not realize it, and that our interactions and
experiences are just as beautiful and awe-inspiring as the growth
and movement of trees.

SOME TREES

John Ashbery

(1927–)

These are amazing: each
Joining a neighbor, as though speech
Were a still performance.
Arranging by chance

To meet as far this morning
From the world as agreeing
With it, you and I
Are suddenly what the trees try

To tell us we are:
That their merely being there
Means something; that soon
We may touch, love, explain.

And glad not to have invented
Some comeliness, we are surrounded:

A silence already filled with noises,
A canvas on which emerges

A chorus of smiles, a winter morning.
Place in a puzzling light, and moving,
Our days put on such reticence
These accents seem their own defense.

THE PRUNED TREE

Howard Moss

(1922–1987)

As a torn paper might seal up its side,
Or a streak of water stitch itself to silk
And disappear, my wound has been my healing,
And I am made more beautiful by losses.
See the flat water in the distance nodding
Approval, the light that fell in love with statues,
Seeing me alive, turn its motion toward me.
Shorn, I rejoice in what was taken from me.

What can the moonlight do with my new shape
But trace and retrace its miracle of order?
I stand, waiting for the strange reaction
Of insects who knew me in my larger self,
Unkempt, in a naturalness I did not love.
Even the dog's voice rings with a new echo,
And all the little leaves I shed are singing,
Singing to the moon of shapely newness.

Somewhere what I lost I hope is springing
To life again. The roofs, astonished by me,
Are taking new bearings in the night, the owl
Is crying for a further wisdom, the lilac
Putting forth its strongest scent to find me.
Butterflies, like sails in grooves, are winging
Out of water to wash me, wash me.
Now, I am stirring like a seed in China.

This poem's sometimes-flowery style expresses a profound truth: the smallest and seemingly least significant things in the world all hold some element of mystery and magic that can transform our experience, if we're willing to take the time to pay attention to them.

HIDDEN JOYS

Laman Blanchard

(1803–1845)

Pleasures lie thickest where no pleasures seem:
There's not a leaf that falls upon the ground
But holds some joy, of silence, or of sound,
Some sprite begotten of a summer dream.
The very meanest things are made supreme
With innate ecstacy. No grain of sand
But moves a bright and million-peopled land,
And hath its Edens and its Eves, I deem.
For Love, though blind himself, a curious eye
Hath lent me, to behold the hearts of things,
And touch'd mine ear with power. Thus, far or nigh,
Minute or mighty, fix'd or free with wings,
Delight from many a nameless covert sly
Peeps sparkling, and in tones familiar sings.

NONSENSE

William Wordsworth was a great poet, but he never exhibited much of a sense of humor. It's enjoyable to speculate what he might have thought of the MAD version of one of his most famous poems (see p. 4), and whether he had any idea of what an axolotl might be (for the curious, it's a kind of Mexican salamander).

I WANDERED LONELY AS A CLOD

The Editors of *MAD* Magazine

I wandered lonely as a clod
Just picking up old rags and bottles,
When onward on my way I plod,
I saw a host of axolotls;
Beside the lake, beneath the trees,
A sight to make a man's blood freeze.

Some had handles, some were plain;
They came in blue, red, pink, and green.
A few were orange in the main;
The damndest sight I've ever seen.
The females gave a sprightly glance;
The male ones all wore knee-length pants.

Now oft, when on the couch I lie,
The doctor asks me what I see.
They flash upon my inward eye
And make me laugh in fiendish glee.
I find my solace then in bottles,
And I forget them axolotls.

The first poem here, one of the comic masterpieces of our litera-
ture, has at its heart a gentle mockery of excessive rationality.
("Logic is logic. That's all I say.") The second is a playful confes-
sion by the poet that he is really too funny to bear! A more seri-
ous, philosophical poem by Holmes appears on p. 180.

THE DEACON'S MASTERPIECE
OR
THE WONDERFUL ONE-HOSS SHAY

Oliver Wendell Holmes

(1809–1894)

Have you heard of the wonderful one-hoss shay,
That was built in such a logical way
It ran a hundred years to a day,
And then, of a sudden, it—ah, but stay,
And I'll tell you what happened without delay,
Scaring the parson into fits,
Frightening people out of their wits,—
Have you ever heard of that, I say?

Seventeen hundred and fifty-five,
Georgius Secundus was then alive,—

Snuffy old drone from the German hive.
That was the year when Lisbon-town
Saw the earth open and gulp her down,
And Braddock's army was done so brown,

Left without a scalp to its crown.
It was on the terrible Earthquake-day
That the Deacon finished the one-hoss shay.
Now in building of chaises, I tell you what,
There is always *somewhere* a weaker spot,—
In hub, tire, felloe, in spring or thill,
In panel, or crossbar, or floor, or sill,
In screw, bolt, thoroughbrace,—lurking still,
Find it somewhere you must and will,—
Above or below, or within or without,—
And that's the reason, beyond a doubt,
A chaise *breaks down,* but doesn't *wear out.*

But the Deacon swore (as Deacons do),
With an "I dew vum," or an "I tell *yeou,*"
He would build one shay to beat the taown
'n' the keounty 'n' all the kentry raoun';
It should be so built that it *couldn'* break daown:
—"Fur," said the Deacon, " 't's mighty plain
Thut the weakes' place mus' stan' the strain;
'n' the way t' fix it, uz I maintain,
Is only jest
T' make that place uz strong uz the rest."

So the Deacon inquired of the village folk
Where he could find the strongest oak,
That couldn't be split nor bent nor broke,—
That was for spokes and floor and sills;
He sent for lancewood to make the thills;
The crossbars were ash, from the straightest trees;
The panels of whitewood, that cuts like cheese,
But lasts like iron for things like these;

The hubs of logs from the "Settler's ellum,"—
Last of its timber,—they couldn't sell 'em,
Never an axe had seen their chips,
And the wedges flew from between their lips,
Their blunt ends frizzled like celery tips;
Step and prop-iron, bolt and screw,
Spring, tire, axle, and linchpin too,
Steel of the finest, bright and blue;
Thoroughbrace bison-skin, thick and wide;
Boot, top, dasher, from tough old hide
Found in the pit when the tanner died.
That was the way he "put her through."—
"There!" said the Deacon, "naow she'll dew!"

Do! I tell you, I rather guess
She was a wonder, and nothing less!
Colts grew horses, beards turned gray,
Deacon and Deaconess dropped away,
Children and grandchildren—where were they?
But there stood the stout old one-hoss shay
As fresh as on Lisbon-earthquake-day!
EIGHTEEN HUNDRED;—it came and found
The Deacon's masterpiece strong and sound.
Eighteen hundred increased by ten;—
"Hahnsum kerridge" they called it then.
Eighteen hundred and twenty came;—
Running as usual; much the same.
Thirty and forty at last arrive,
And then came fifty, and FIFTY-FIVE,

Little of all we value here
Wakes on the morn of its hundredth year

Without both feeling and looking queer.
In fact, there's nothing that keeps its youth,
So far as I know, but a tree and truth.
(This as a moral that runs at large;
Take it,—You're welcome.—No extra charge.)

FIRST OF NOVEMBER—the-Earthquake-day.—
There are traces of age in the one-hoss shay,
A general flavor of mild decay,
But nothing local, as one may say.
There couldn't be,—for the Deacon's art
Had made it so like in every part
That there wasn't a chance for one to start.
For the wheels were just as strong as the thills,
And the floor was just as strong as the sills,
And the panels just as strong as the floor,
And the whippletree neither less nor more,
And the back-crossbar as strong as the fore,
And spring and axle and hub *encore,*
And yet, *as a whole,* it is past a doubt
In another hour it will be *worn out!*

First of November, 'Fifty-five!
This morning the parson takes a drive.
Now, small boys, get out of the way!
Here comes the wonderful one-hoss shay,
Drawn by a rat-tailed, ewe-necked bay.
"Huddup!" said the parson.—Off went they.
The parson was working his Sunday's text,—
Had got to *fifthly,* and stopped perplexed
At what the—Moses—was coming next.
All at once the horse stood still,

Close by the meet'n'-house on the hill.
First a shiver, and then a thrill,
Then something decidedly like a spill,—
And the parson was sitting upon a rock,
At half-past nine by the meet'n'-house clock,—
Just the hour of the Earthquake shock!
—What do you think the parson found,
When he got up and stared around?
The poor old chaise in a heap or mound,
As if it had been to the mill and ground!
You see, of course, if you're not a dunce,
How it went to pieces all at once,—
All at once, and nothing first,—
Just as bubbles do when they burst.

End of the wonderful one-hoss shay.
Logic is logic. That's all I say.

THE HEIGHT OF THE RIDICULOUS

Oliver Wendell Holmes

(1809–1894)

I wrote some lines once on a time
   In wondrous merry mood,
And thought, as usual, men would say
   They were exceeding good.

They were so queer, so very queer,
   I laughed as I would die;
Albeit, in the general way,
   A sober man am I.

I called my servant, and he came;
   How kind it was of him
To mind a slender man like me,
   He of the mighty limb.

"These to the printer," I exclaimed,
   And, in my humorous way,
I added (as a trifling jest,)
   "There'll be the devil to pay."

He took the paper, and I watched,
   And saw him peep within;
At the first line he read, his face
   Was all upon the grin.

He read the next; the grin grew broad,
    And shot from ear to ear;
He read the third; a chuckling noise
    I now began to hear.

The fourth; he broke into a roar;
    The fifth; his waistband split;
The sixth; he burst five buttons off,
    And tumbled in a fit.

Ten days and nights, with sleepless eye,
    I watched that wretched man,
And since, I never dare to write
    As funny as I can.

When you think of nonsense poetry that somehow seems to make sense, Lewis Carroll inevitably comes to mind. "Jabberwocky" is a mock epic filled with words that seem to mean something, except they're indefinable! When reading the second poem, it's good to remember that it's recited—sung, really—by a creature called the Mock Turtle, praising the soup of the same name.

JABBERWOCKY

Lewis Carroll

(1832–1898)

'Twas brillig, and the slithy toves
    Did gyre and gimble in the wabe:
All mimsy were the borogoves,
    And the mome raths outgrabe.

"Beware the Jabberwock, my son!
    The jaws that bite, the claws that catch!
Beware the Jubjub bird, and shun
    The frumious Bandersnatch!"

He took his vorpal sword in hand:
    Long time the manxome foe he sought—
So rested he by the Tumtum tree,
    And stood awhile in thought.

And, as in uffish thought he stood,
    The Jabberwock, with eyes of flame,

Came whiffling through the tulgey wood,
    And burbled as it came!

One, two! One, two! And through and through
    The vorpal blade went snicker-snack!
He left it dead, and with its head
    He went galumphing back.

"And, hast thou slain the Jabberwock?
    Come to my arms, my beamish boy!
O frabjous day! Callooh! Callay!"
    He chortled in his joy.

'Twas brillig, and the slithy toves
    Did gyre and gimble in the wabe;
All mimsy were the borogoves,
    And the mome raths outgrabe.

BEAUTIFUL SOUP

Lewis Carroll

(1832–1898)

Beautiful Soup, so rich and green,
Waiting in a hot tureen!
Who for such dainties would not stoop?
Soup of the evening, beautiful Soup!
Soup of the evening, beautiful Soup!

Beau—ootiful Soo-oop!
Beau—ootiful Soo-oop!
Soo—oop of the e—e—evening,
Beautiful, beautiful Soup!

Beautiful Soup! Who cares for fish,
Game, or any other dish?
Who would not give all else for two p
Ennyworth only of beautiful Soup?
Pennyworth only of beautiful Soup?

Beau—ootiful Soo-oop!
Beau—ootiful Soo-oop!
Soo—oop of the e—e—evening,
Beautiful, beauti—FUL SOUP!

Gilbert and Sullivan patter songs are meant to be sung (or recited) as quickly and with as much dexterity in pronunciation as possible. The two below, the first from the operetta The Sorcerer *and the other from* The Pirates of Penzance, *are as much fun to recite as to listen to.*

THE SORCERER'S SONG

W. S. Gilbert

(1836–1911)

Oh! My name is John Wellington Wells—
I'm a dealer in magic and spells,
In blessings and curses,
And ever-filled purses,
In prophecies, witches, and knells!
If you want a proud foe to make tracks—
If you'd melt a rich uncle in wax—
You've but to look in
On our resident Djinn,
Number seventy, Simmery Axe!

We've a first-class assortment of magic;
And for raising a posthumous shade
With effects that are comic or tragic,
There's no cheaper house in the trade.
Love-philtre—we've quantities of it;
And for knowledge if anyone burns,
We're keeping a very small prophet, a prophet
Who brings us unbounded returns:

For he can prophesy
With a wink of his eye,
Peep with security
Into futurity,
Sum up your history,
Clear up a mystery,
Humour proclivity
For a nativity—for a nativity;
He has answers oracular,
Bogies spectacular,
Tetrapods tragical,
Mirrors so magical,
Facts astronomical,
Solemn or comical,
And, if you want it, he
Makes a reduction on taking a quantity!

Oh! If anyone anything lacks,
He'll find it all ready in stacks,
If he'll only look in
On the resident Djinn,
Number seventy, Simmery Axe!

He can raise you hosts,
Of ghosts,
And that without reflectors;
And creepy things
With wings,
And gaunt and grisly spectres!
He can fill you crowds
Of shrouds,
And horrify you vastly;

He can rack your brains
With chains,
And gibberings grim and ghastly.

Then, if you plan it, he
Changes organity
With an urbanity,
Full of Satanity,
Vexes humanity
With an inanity
Fatal to vanity—
Driving your foes to the verge of insanity.

Barring tautology,
In demonology,
'Lectro biology,
Mystic nosology,
Spirit philology,
High class astrology,
Such is his knowledge, he
Isn't the man to require an apology!

Oh! My name is John Wellington Wells—
I'm a dealer in magic and spells,
In blessings and curses,
And ever-filled purses—
In prophecies, witches, and knells.
If anyone anything lacks,
He'll find it all ready in stacks,
If he'll only look in
On the resident Djinn,
Number seventy, Simmery Axe!

I AM THE VERY MODEL OF A MODERN MAJOR-GENERAL

W. S. Gilbert

(1836–1911)

I am the very model of a modern Major-General
I've information vegetable, animal, and mineral
I know the kings of England, and I quote the fights
historical
From Marathon to Waterloo, in order categorical;

I'm very well acquainted, too, with matters mathematical,
I understand equations, both the simple and quadratical,
About binomial theorem I'm teeming with a lot o' news,
With many cheerful facts about the square of the
hypotenuse.

With many cheerful facts about the square of the hypotenuse,
With many cheerful facts about the square of the hypotenuse,
With many cheerful facts about the square of the
hypoten-potenuse.

I'm very good at integral and differential calculus;
I know the scientific names of beings animalculous;
In short, in matters vegetable, animal, and mineral,
I am the very model of a modern Major-General.

In short, in matters vegetable, animal, and mineral,
He is the very model of a modern Major-General.

I know our mythic history, King Arthur's and Sir Caradoc's;
I answer hard acrostics, I've a pretty taste for paradox,
I quote in elegiacs all the crimes of Heliogabalus,
In conics I can floor peculiarities parabolous;

I can tell undoubted Raphaels from Gerard Dows and
    Zoffanies,
I know the croaking chorus from the *Frogs* of Aristophanes!
Then I can hum a fugue of which I've heard the music's din
    afore,
And whistle all the airs from that infernal nonsense
    Pinafore.

And whistle all the airs from that infernal nonsense Pinafore,
And whistle all the airs from that infernal nonsense Pinafore,
And whistle all the airs from that infernal nonsense
    Pina-Pinafore.

Then I can write a washing bill in Babylonic cuneiform,
And tell you ev'ry detail of Caractacus's uniform:
In short, in matters vegetable, animal, and mineral,
I am the very model of a modern Major-General.

In short, in matters vegetable, animal, and mineral,
He is the very model of a modern Major-General.

In fact, when I know what is meant by "mamelon" and
    "ravelin,"
When I can tell at sight a Mauser rifle from a javelin,
When such affairs as sorties and surprises I'm more wary at,
And when I know precisely what is meant by
    "commissariat,"

When I have learnt what progress has been made in modern
    gunnery,
When I know more of tactics than a novice in a nunnery;
In short, when I've a smattering of elemental strategy,
You'll say a better Major-General had never sat a gee.

You'll say a better Major-General had never sat a gee,
You'll say a better Major-General had never sat a gee,
You'll say a better Major-General had never sat a, sat a gee.

For my military knowledge, though I'm plucky and
    adventury,
Has only been brought down to the beginning of the
    century;
But still, in matters vegetable, animal, and mineral,
I am the very model of a modern Major-General.

But still, in matters vegetable, animal, and mineral,
He is the very model of a modern Major-General.

Lear was the youngest of twenty-one children and so presumably had an early acquaintance with nursery rhymes and nonsense verse (he was, among other things, a popularizer of the limerick). His accounts of the Jumblies and the Pobble rise to the highest level of the nonsensical, which is that they seem less to be written than to have always existed in some part of our collective unconscious.

THE JUMBLIES

Edward Lear

(1812–1888)

I

They went to sea in a Sieve, they did,
   In a Sieve they went to sea:
In spite of all their friends could say,
On a winter's morn, on a stormy day,
   In a Sieve they went to sea!
And when the Sieve turned round and round,
And every one cried, 'You'll all be drowned!'
They called aloud, 'Our Sieve ain't big,
But we don't care a button! we don't care a fig!
   In a Sieve we'll go to sea!'
     Far and few, far and few,
       Are the lands where the Jumblies live;
      Their heads are green, and their hands are blue,
        And they went to sea in a Sieve.

II

They sailed away in a Sieve, they did,
In a Sieve they sailed so fast,
  With only a beautiful pea-green veil
Tied with a riband by way of a sail,
  To a small tobacco-pipe mast;
And every one said, who saw them go,
'O won't they be soon upset, you know!
For the sky is dark, and the voyage is long,
And happen what may, it's extremely wrong
  In a Sieve to sail so fast!'
    Far and few, far and few,
      Are the lands where the Jumblies live;
      Their heads are green, and their hands are blue,
      And they went to sea in a Sieve.

III

The water it soon came in, it did,
  The water it soon came in;
So to keep them dry, they wrapped their feet
In a pinky paper all folded neat,
  And they fastened it down with a pin.
And they passed the night in a crockery-jar,
And each of them said, 'How wise we are!
Though the sky be dark, and the voyage be long,
Yet we never can think we were rash or wrong,
  While round in our Sieve we spin!'
    Far and few, far and few,
      Are the lands where the Jumblies live;
      Their heads are green, and their hands are blue,
      And they went to sea in a Sieve.

IV

And all night long they sailed away;
    And when the sun went down,
They whistled and warbled a moony song
To the echoing sound of a coppery gong,
    In the shade of the mountains brown.
'O Timballo! How happy we are,
When we live in a Sieve and a crockery-jar,
And all night long in the moonlight pale,
We sail away with a pea-green sail,
    In the shade of the mountains brown!'
      Far and few, far and few,
        Are the lands where the Jumblies live;
      Their heads are green, and their hands are blue,
        And they went to sea in a Sieve.

V

They sailed to the Western Sea, they did,
    To a land all covered with trees,
And they bought an Owl, and a useful Cart,
And a pound of Rice, and a Cranberry Tart,
    And a hive of silvery Bees.
And they bought a Pig, and some green Jack-daws,
And a lovely Monkey with lollipop paws,
And forty bottles of Ring-Bo-Ree,
    And no end of Stilton Cheese.
      Far and few, far and few,
        Are the lands where the Jumblies live;
      Their heads are green, and their hands are blue,
        And they went to sea in a Sieve.

VI

And in twenty years they all came back,
   In twenty years or more,
And every one said, 'How tall they've grown!
For they've been to the Lakes, and the Torrible Zone,
   And the hills of the Chankly Bore!'
And they drank their health, and gave them a feast
Of dumplings made of beautiful yeast;
And every one said, 'If we only live,
We too will go to sea in a Sieve,—
   To the hills of the Chankly Bore!'
     Far and few, far and few,
       Are the lands where the Jumblies live;
      Their heads are green, and their hands are blue,
        And they went to sea in a Sieve.

THE POBBLE WHO HAS NO TOES

Edward Lear

(1812–1888)

The Pobble who has no toes
Had once as many as we;
When they said "Some day you may lose them all;"
He replied "Fish, fiddle-de-dee!"
And his Aunt Jobiska made him drink
Lavender water tinged with pink,
For she said "The World in general knows
There's nothing so good for a Pobble's toes!"

The Pobble who has no toes
Swam across the Bristol Channel;
But before he set out he wrapped his nose
In a piece of scarlet flannel.
For his Aunt Jobiska said "No harm
Can come to his toes if his nose is warm;
And it's perfectly known that a Pobble's toes
Are safe,—provided he minds his nose!"

The Pobble swam fast and well,
And when boats or ships came near him,
He tinkledy-blinkledy-winkled a bell,
So that all the world could hear him.
And all the Sailors and Admirals cried,
When they saw him nearing the further side—
"He has gone to fish for his Aunt Jobiska's
Runcible Cat with crimson whiskers!"

But before he touched the shore,
The shore of the Bristol Channel,
A sea-green porpoise carried away
His wrapper of scarlet flannel.
And when he came to observe his feet,
Formerly garnished with toes so neat,
His face at once became forlorn,
On perceiving that all his toes were gone!

And nobody ever knew,
From that dark day to the present,
Whoso had taken the Pobble's toes,
In a manner so far from pleasant.
Whether the shrimps, or crawfish grey,
Or crafty Mermaids stole them away—
Nobody knew: and nobody knows
How the Pobble was robbed of his twice five toes!

The Pobble who has no toes
Was placed in a friendly Bark,
And they rowed him back, and carried him up
To his Aunt Jobiska's Park.
And she made him a feast at his earnest wish
Of eggs and buttercups fried with fish,—
And she said—"It's a fact the whole world knows,
That Pobbles are happier without their toes!"

Dreams offer an escape from reality, a place where one's most incredible fantasies can take shape. Eugene Field was the father of eight children and perhaps he recited these poems to them at bedtime so they would drift into worlds where their imagination would blossom.

WYNKEN, BLYNKEN, AND NOD

Eugene Field

(1850–1895)

Wynken, Blynken and Nod one night
Sailed off in a wooden shoe,
Sailed on a river of crystal light
Into a sea of dew

Where are you going
And what do you wish
The old man asked the three
We've come to fish
For the herring fish
That swim in the beautiful sea
Nets of silver and gold have we
Said Wynken, Blynken and Nod

So all night long
Their nets they threw
To the stars in the twinklin' foam
Then down from the sky
Came the wooden shoe
Bringing the fishermen home

'Twas oh so pretty
A sail it seemed
As if it could not be
And some folks thought
'Twas a dream they'd dreamed
Of sailing the beautiful sea
But I shall name you
The fishermen three
Wynken, Blynken and Nod

Wynken and Blynken
Are two little eyes
And Nod is a weary head
And the wooden shoe
That sailed the skies
Is a wee one's trundle bed
So shut your eyes
While Mommy sings
Of the wonderful sights that be
And you shall see
All the beautiful things
As you rock in that misty sea
Just like the fishermen three
Wynken, Blynken and Nod
Just like the fishermen three
Wynken, Blynken and Nod

THE SUGAR-PLUM TREE

Eugene Field
(1850–1895)

Have you ever heard of the Sugar-Plum Tree?
    'T is a marvel of great renown!
It blooms on the shore of the Lollipop sea
    In the garden of Shut-Eye Town;
The fruit that it bears is so wondrously sweet
    (As those who have tasted it say)
That good little children have only to eat
    Of that fruit to be happy next day.

When you've got to the tree, you would have a hard time
    To capture the fruit which I sing;
The tree is so tall that no person could climb
    To the boughs where the sugar-plums swing!
But up in that tree sits a chocolate cat,
    And a gingerbread dog prowls below—
And this is the way you contrive to get at
    Those sugar-plums tempting you so:

You say but the word to that gingerbread dog
    And he barks with such terrible zest
That the chocolate cat is at once all agog,
    As her swelling proportions attest.
And the chocolate cat goes cavorting around
    From this leafy limb unto that,
And the sugar-plums tumble, of course, to the ground—
    Hurrah for that chocolate cat!

There are marshmallows, gumdrops, and peppermint canes,
    With stripings of scarlet or gold,
And you carry away of the treasure that rains
    As much as your apron can hold!
So come, little child, cuddle closer to me
    In your dainty white nightcap and gown,
And I'll rock you away to that Sugar-Plum Tree
    In the garden of Shut-Eye Town.

T. S. Eliot depicts an assortment of hilarious feline characters with very human idiosyncrasies in his book of verse for children, Old Possum's Book of Practical Cats, *which includes the following poems. These colorful characters eventually starred in* Cats, *the highly acclaimed musical based on Eliot's book.*

GUS: THE THEATRE CAT

T. S. Eliot
(1888–1965)

Gus is the Cat at the Theatre Door.
His name, as I ought to have told you before,
Is really Asparagus. That's such a fuss
To pronounce, that we usually call him just Gus.
His coat's very shabby, he's thin as a rake,
And he suffers from palsy that makes his paw shake.
Yet he was, in his youth, quite the smartest of Cats—
But no longer a terror to mice and to rats.
For he isn't the Cat that he was in his prime;
Though his name was quite famous, he says, in its time.
And whenever he joins his friends at their club
(Which takes place at the back of the neighbouring pub)
He loves to regale them, if someone else pays,
With anecdotes drawn from his palmiest days.
For he once was a Star of the highest degree—
He has acted with Irving, he's acted with Tree.
And he likes to relate his success on the Halls,
Where the Gallery once gave him seven cat-calls.

But his grandest creation, as he loves to tell,
Was Firefrorefiddle, the Fiend of the Fell.

"I have played," so he says, "every possible part,
And I used to know seventy speeches by heart.
I'd extemporize back-chat, I knew how to gag,
And I knew how to let the cat out of the bag.
I knew how to act with my back and my tail;
With an hour of rehearsal, I never could fail.
I'd a voice that would soften the hardest of hearts,
Whether I took the lead, or in character parts.
I have sat by the bedside of poor Little Nell;
When the Curfew was rung, then I swung on the bell.
In the Pantomime season I never fell flat,
And I once understudied Dick Whittington's Cat.
But my grandest creation, as history will tell,
Was Firefrorefiddle, the Fiend of the Fell."

Then, if someone will give him a toothful of gin,
He will tell how he once played a part in *East Lynne*.
At a Shakespeare performance he once walked on pat,
When some actor suggested the need for a cat.
He once played a Tiger—could do it again—
Which an Indian Colonel pursued down a drain.
And he thinks that he still can, much better than most,
Produce blood-curdling noises to bring on the Ghost.
And he once crossed the stage on a telegraph wire,
To rescue a child when a house was on fire.
And he says: "Now these kittens, they do not get trained
As we did in the days when Victoria reigned.
They never get drilled in a regular troupe,

And they think they are smart, just to jump through a hoop."
And he'll say, as he scratches himself with his claws,
"Well, the Theatre's certainly not what it was.
These modern productions are all very well,
But there's nothing to equal, from what I hear tell,
That moment of mystery
When I made history
As Firefrorefiddle, the Fiend of the Fell."

THE OLD GUMBIE CAT

T. S. Eliot
(1888–1965)

I have a Gumbie Cat in mind, her name is Jennyanydots;
Her coat is of the tabby kind, with tiger stripes and leopard
　spots.
All day she sits upon the stair or on the steps or on the mat;
She sits and sits and sits and sits—and that's what makes a
　Gumbie Cat!

But when the day's hustle and bustle is done,
Then the Gumbie Cat's work is but hardly begun.
And when all the family's in bed and asleep,
She tucks up her skirts to the basement to creep.
She is deeply concerned with the ways of the mice—
Their behaviour's not good and their manners not nice;
So when she has got them lined up on the matting,
She teachs them music, crocheting and tatting.

I have a Gumbie Cat in mind, her name is Jennyanydots;
Her equal would be hard to find, she likes the warm and
　sunny spots.
All day she sits beside the hearth or on the bed or on my
　hat:
She sits and sits and sits and sits—and that's what makes a
　Gumbie Cat!

But when the day's hustle and bustle is done,
Then the Gumbie Cat's work is but hardly begun.

As she finds that the mice will not ever keep quiet,
She is sure it is due to irregular diet;
And believing that nothing is done without trying,
She sets right to work with her baking and frying.
She makes them a mouse-cake of bread and dried peas,
And a beautiful fry of lean bacon and cheese.

I have a Gumbie Cat in mind, her name is Jennyanydots;
The curtain-cord she likes to wind, and tie it into sailor-
    knots.
She sits upon the window-sill, or anything that's smooth
    and flat:
She sits and sits and sits and sits—and that's what makes a
    Gumbie Cat!

But when the day's hustle and bustle is done,
Then the Gumbie Cat's work is but hardly begun.
She thinks that the cockroaches just need employment
To prevent them from idle and wanton destroyment.
So she's formed, from that lot of disorderly louts,
A troop of well-disciplined helpful boy-scouts,
With a purpose in life and a good deed to do—
And she's even created a Beetles' Tattoo.

So for Old Gumbie Cats let us now give three cheers—
On whom well-ordered households depend, it appears.

Shel Silverstein wrote poetry and books for children, but his work can be appreciated by people of all ages. In poetry and prose, Silverstein invites his readers to be swept away from their everyday lives to wondrous places, where the impossible becomes delightfully possible.

WHERE THE SIDEWALK ENDS

Shel Silverstein
(1932–1999)

There is a place where the sidewalk ends
And before the street begins,
And there the grass grows soft and white,
And there the sun burns crimson bright,
And there the moon-bird rests from his flight
To cool in the peppermint wind.

Let us leave this place where the smoke blows black
And the dark street winds and bends.
Past the pits where the asphalt flowers grow
We shall walk with a walk that is measured and slow,
And watch where the chalk-white arrows go
To the place where the sidewalk ends.

Yes we'll walk with a walk that is measured and slow,
And we'll go where the chalk-white arrows go,
For the children, they mark, and the children, they know
The place where the sidewalk ends.

MELINDA MAE

Shel Silverstein

(1932–1999)

Have you heard of tiny Melinda Mae,
Who ate a monstrous whale?
She thought she could,
She said she would,
So she started in right at the tail.
And everyone said, "You're much too small,"
But that didn't bother Melinda at all,
She took little bites and she chewed very slow,
Just like a little girl should . . .

. . . and eighty-nine years later she ate that whale
Because she said she would!!!

Ogden Nash's daughter Isabel was the inspiration for the clever young girl in the following poem. The most terrifying opponents are no match for Isabel, and her unwavering determination resonates with Shel Silverstein's Melinda Mae, who resolves to eat an entire whale despite the odds (p. 82).

THE ADVENTURES OF ISABEL

Ogden Nash
(1902–1971)

Isabel met an enormous bear,
Isabel, Isabel, didn't care;
The bear was hungry, the bear was ravenous,
The bear's big mouth was cruel and cavernous.
The bear said, Isabel, glad to meet you,
How do, Isabel, now I'll eat you!
Isabel, Isabel, didn't worry.
Isabel didn't scream or scurry.
She washed her hands and she straightened her hair up,
Then Isabel quietly ate the bear up.

Once in a night as black as pitch
Isabel met a wicked old witch.
The witch's face was cross and wrinkled,
The witch's gums with teeth were sprinkled.
Ho, ho, Isabel! the old witch crowed,
I'll turn you into an ugly toad!
Isabel, Isabel, didn't worry,

Isabel didn't scream or scurry,
She showed no rage and she showed no rancor,
But she turned the witch into milk and drank her.

Isabel met a hideous giant,
Isabel continued self reliant.
The giant was hairy, the giant was horrid,
He had one eye in the middle of his forehead.
Good morning, Isabel, the giant said,
I'll grind your bones to make my bread.
Isabel, Isabel, didn't worry,
Isabel didn't scream or scurry.
She nibbled the zwieback that she always fed off,
And when it was gone, she cut the giant's head off.

Isabel met a troublesome doctor,
He punched and he poked till he really shocked her.
The doctor's talk was of coughs and chills
And the doctor's satchel bulged with pills.
The doctor said unto Isabel,
Swallow this, it will make you well.
Isabel, Isabel, didn't worry,
Isabel didn't scream or scurry.
She took those pills from the pill concocter,
And Isabel calmly cured the doctor.

While he worked as a solicitor in Sydney, Australia, Banjo Paterson longed to return to the countryside where he had grown up. Paterson's daydreams of rural Australia eventually became the inspiration for his poetry. The following poems capture the rebellious and fun-loving spirit of people who lived in the outback.

MULGA BILL'S BICYCLE

Banjo Paterson
(1864–1941)

'Twas Mulga Bill, from Eaglehawk, that caught the cycling craze;
He turned away the good old horse that served him many days;
He dressed himself in cycling clothes, resplendent to be seen;
He hurried off to town and bought a shining new machine;
And as he wheeled it through the door, with air of lordly pride,
The grinning shop assistant said, "Excuse me, can you ride?"

"See, here, young man," said Mulga Bill, "from Walgett to the sea,
From Conroy's Gap to Castlereagh, there's none can ride like me.
I'm good all round at everything, as everybody knows,
Although I'm not the one to talk—I hate a man that blows.
But riding is my special gift, my chiefest, sole delight;

Just ask a wild duck can it swim, a wild cat can it fight.
There's nothing clothed in hair or hide, or built of flesh or
    steel,
There's nothing walks or jumps, or runs, on axle, hoof, or
    wheel,
But what I'll sit, while hide will hold and girths and straps
    are tight:
I'll ride this here two-wheeled concern right straight away
    at sight."

'Twas Mulga Bill, from Eaglehawk, that sought his own
    abode,
That perched above the Dead Man's Creek, beside the
    mountain road.
He turned the cycle down the hill and mounted for the fray,
But ere he'd gone a dozen yards it bolted clean away.
It left the track, and through the trees, just like a silver
    streak,
It whistled down the awful slope, towards the Dead Man's
    Creek.

It shaved a stump by half an inch, it dodged a big white-box:
The very wallaroos in fright went scrambling up the rocks,
The wombats hiding in their caves dug deeper
    underground,
As Mulga Bill, as white as chalk, sat tight to every bound.
It struck a stone and gave a spring that cleared a fallen tree,
It raced beside a precipice as close as close could be;
And then as Mulga Bill let out one last despairing shriek
It made a leap of twenty feet into the Dead Man's Creek.

'Twas Mulga Bill, from Eaglehawk, that slowly swam ashore:
He said, "I've had some narrer shaves and lively rides before;
I've rode a wild bull round a yard to win a five-pound bet,
But this was the most awful ride that I've encountered yet.
I'll give that two-wheeled outlaw best; it's shaken all my
    nerve
To feel it whistle through the air and plunge and buck and
    swerve.
It's safe at rest in Dead Man's Creek, we'll leave it lying still;
A horse's back is good enough henceforth for Mulga Bill."

THE MAN FROM IRONBARK

Banjo Paterson

(1864–1941)

It was the man from Ironbark who struck the Sydney town,
He wandered over street and park, he wandered up and
  down.
He loitered here, he loitered there, till he was like to drop,
Until at last in sheer despair he sought a barber's shop.
" 'Ere! shave my beard and whiskers off, I'll be a man of
  mark,
I'll go and do the Sydney toff up home in Ironbark."

The barber man was small and flash, as barbers mostly are,
He wore a strike-your-fancy sash, he smoked a huge cigar;
He was a humorist of note and keen at repartee,
He laid the odds and kept a "tote," whatever that may be,
And when he saw our friend arrive, he whispered, "Here's a
  lark!
Just watch me catch him all alive, this man from Ironbark."

There were some gilded youths that sat along the barber's
  wall.
Their eyes were dull, their heads were flat, they had no
  brains at all;
To them the barber passed the wink, his dexter eyelid shut,
"I'll make this bloomin' yokel think his bloomin' throat is
  cut."
And as he soaped and rubbed it in he made a rude remark:
"I s'pose the flats is pretty green up there in Ironbark."

A grunt was all reply he got; he shaved the bushman's chin,
Then made the water boiling hot and dipped the razor in.
He raised his hand, his brow grew black, he paused awhile
to gloat,
Then slashed the red-hot razor-back across his victim's
throat:
Upon the newly-shaven skin it made a livid mark—
No doubt it fairly took him in—the man from Ironbark.

He fetched a wild up-country yell might wake the dead to
hear,
And though his throat, he knew full well, was cut from ear
to ear,
He struggled gamely to his feet, and faced the murd'rous
foe:
"You've done for me! you dog, I'm beat! one hit before I go!
I only wish I had a knife, you blessed murdering shark!
But you'll remember all your life the man from Ironbark."

He lifted up his hairy paw, with one tremendous clout
He landed on the barber's jaw, and knocked the barber out.
He set to work with nail and tooth, he made the place a wreck;
He grabbed the nearest gilded youth, and tried to break his
neck.
And all the while his throat he held to save his vital spark,
And "Murder! Bloody murder!" yelled the man from
Ironbark.

A peeler man who heard the din came in to see the show;
He tried to run the bushman in, but he refused to go.
And when at last the barber spoke, and said " 'Twas all in
fun—

'Twas just a little harmless joke, a trifle overdone."
"A joke!" he cried, "By George, that's fine; a lively sort of
    lark;
I'd like to catch that murdering swine some night in
    Ironbark."

And now while round the shearing floor the list'ning
    shearers gape,
He tells the story o'er and o'er, and brags of his escape.
"Them barber chaps what keeps a tote, By George, I've had
    enough,
One tried to cut my bloomin' throat, but thank the Lord it's
    tough."
And whether he's believed or no, there's one thing to
    remark,
That flowing beards are all the go way up in Ironbark.

Robert Service was born in England and grew up in Scotland, but it wasn't until he moved to a small town in Canada that he discovered the extraordinary people who would become characters in his poetry. The following poems depict the colorful folk one might have encountered if one ventured as far north as the Yukon Territory during the early twentieth century.

THE CREMATION OF SAM McGEE

Robert Service
(1874–1958)

There are strange things done in the midnight sun
By the men who moil for gold;
The Arctic trails have their secret tales
That would make your blood run cold;
The Northern Lights have seen queer sights,
But the queerest they ever did see
Was that night on the marge of Lake Lebarge
I cremated Sam McGee.

Now Sam McGee was from Tennessee, where the cotton
   blooms and blows.
Why he left his home in the South to roam 'round the Pole,
   God only knows.
He was always cold, but the land of gold seemed to hold
   him like a spell;
Though he'd often say in his homely way that "he'd sooner
   live in hell."

On a Christmas Day we were mushing our way over the
Dawson trail.
Talk of your cold! through the parka's fold it stabbed like a
driven nail.
If our eyes we'd close, then the lashes froze till sometimes
we couldn't see;
It wasn't much fun, but the only one to whimper was Sam
McGee.

And that very night, as we lay packed tight in our robes
beneath the snow,
And the dogs were fed, and the stars o'erhead were dancing
heel and toe,
He turned to me, and "Cap," says he, "I'll cash in this trip,
I guess;
And if I do, I'm asking that you won't refuse my last
request."

Well, he seemed so low that I couldn't say no; then he says
with a sort of moan:
"It's the cursèd cold, and it's got right hold till I'm chilled
clean through to the bone.
Yet 'taint being dead—it's my awful dread of the icy grave
that pains;
So I want you to swear that, foul or fair, you'll cremate my
last remains."

A pal's last need is a thing to heed, so I swore I would not
fail;
And we started on at the streak of dawn; but God! he looked
ghastly pale.

He crouched on the sleigh, and he raved all day of his home
in Tennessee;
And before nightfall a corpse was all that was left of Sam
McGee.

There wasn't a breath in that land of death, and I hurried,
horror-driven,
With a corpse half hid that I couldn't get rid, because of a
promise given;
It was lashed to the sleigh, and it seemed to say: "You may
tax your brawn and brains,
But you promised true, and it's up to you to cremate those
last remains."

Now a promise made is a debt unpaid, and the trail has its
own stern code.
In the days to come, though my lips were dumb, in my heart
how I cursed that load.
In the long, long night, by the lone firelight, while the
huskies, round in a ring,
Howled out their woes to the homeless snows—O God!
how I loathed the thing.

And every day that quiet clay seemed to heavy and heavier
grow;
And on I went, though the dogs were spent and the grub
was getting low;
The trail was bad, and I felt half mad, but I swore I would
not give in;
And I'd often sing to the hateful thing, and it hearkened
with a grin.

Till I came to the marge of Lake Lebarge, and a derelict
  there lay;
It was jammed in the ice, but I saw in a trice it was called the
  "Alice May."
And I looked at it, and I thought a bit, and I looked at my
  frozen chum;
Then "Here," said I, with a sudden cry, "is my cre-ma-tor-
  eum."

Some planks I tore from the cabin floor, and I lit the boiler
  fire;
Some coal I found that was lying around, and I heaped the
  fuel higher;
The flames just soared and the furnace roared—such a
  blaze you seldom see;
Then I burrowed a hole in the glowing coal, and I stuffed in
  Sam McGee.

Then I made a hike, for I didn't like to hear him sizzle so;
And the heavens scowled, and the huskies howled, and the
  wind began to blow.
It was icy cold, but the hot sweat rolled down my cheeks,
  and I don't know why;
And the greasy smoke in an inky cloak went streaking down
  the sky.

I do not know how long in the snow I wrestled with grisly
  fear;
But the stars came out and they danced about ere again I
  ventured near;
I was sick with dread, but I bravely said: "I'll just take a peep
  inside.

I guess he's cooked, and it's time I looked;"... then the door
    I opened wide.

And there sat Sam, looking cool and calm, in the heart of
    the furnace roar;
And he wore a smile you could see a mile, and he said:
    "Please close that door.
It's fine in here, but I greatly fear you'll let in the cold and
    storm—
Since I left Plumtree, down in Tennessee, it's the first time
    I've been warm."

There are strange things done in the midnight sun
By the men who moil for gold;
The Arctic trails have their secret tales
That would make your blood run cold;
The Northern Lights have seen queer sights,
But the queerest they ever did see
Was that night on the marge of Lake Lebarge
I cremated Sam McGee.

THE SHOOTING OF DAN McGREW

Robert Service

(1874–1958)

A bunch of the boys were whooping it up in the Malamute
    saloon;
The kid that handles the music-box was hitting a jag-time
    tune;
Back of the bar, in a solo game, sat Dangerous Dan
    McGrew,
And watching his luck was his light-o'-love, the lady that's
    known as Lou.

When out of the night, which was fifty below, and into the
    din and the glare,
There stumbled a miner fresh from the creeks, dog-dirty,
    and loaded for bear.
He looked like a man with a foot in the grave and scarcely
    the strength of a louse,
Yet he tilted a poke of dust on the bar, and he called for
    drinks for the house.
There was none could place the stranger's face, though we
    searched ourselves for a clue;
But we drank his health, and the last to drink was
    Dangerous Dan McGrew.

There's men that somehow just grip your eyes, and hold
    them hard like a spell;
And such was he, and he looked to me like a man who had
    lived in hell;

With a face most hair, and the dreary stare of a dog whose
    day is done,
As he watered the green stuff in his glass, and the drops fell
    one by one.
Then I got to figgering who he was, and wondering what
    he'd do,
And I turned my head—and there watching him was the
    lady that's known as Lou.

His eyes went rubbering round the room, and he seemed in
    a kind of daze,
Till at last that old piano fell in the way of his wandering
    gaze.
The rag-time kid was having a drink; there was no one else
    on the stool,
So the stranger stumbles across the room, and flops down
    there like a fool.
In a buckskin shirt that was glazed with dirt he sat, and I
    saw him sway;
Then he clutched the keys with his talon hands—my God!
    but that man could play.

Were you ever out in the Great Alone, when the moon was
    awful clear,
And the icy mountains hemmed you in with a silence you
    most could *hear*;
With only the howl of a timber wolf, and you camped there
    in the cold,
A half-dead thing in a stark, dead world, clean mad for the
    muck called gold;
While high overhead, green, yellow and red, the North
    Lights swept in bars?—

Then you've a haunch what the music meant . . . hunger and
    might and the stars.

And hunger not of the belly kind, that's banished with
    bacon and beans,
But the gnawing hunger of lonely men for a home and all
    that it means;
For a fireside far from the cares that are, four walls and a
    roof above;
But oh! so cramful of cosy joy, and crowned with a woman's
    love—
A woman dearer than all the world, and true as Heaven is
    true—
(God! how ghastly she looks through her rouge,—the lady
    that's known as Lou.)

Then on a sudden the music changed, so soft that you
    scarce could hear;
But you felt that your life had been looted clean of all that it
    once held dear;
That someone had stolen the woman you loved; that her
    love was a devil's lie;
That your guts were gone, and the best for you was to crawl
    away and die.
'Twas the crowning cry of a heart's despair, and it thrilled
    you through and through—
"I guess I'll make it a spread misere," said Dangerous Dan
    McGrew.

The music almost died away . . . then it burst like a pent-up
    flood;
And it seemed to say, "Repay, repay," and my eyes were blind
    with blood.
The thought came back of an ancient wrong, and it stung
    like a frozen lash,
And the lust awoke to kill, to kill . . . then the music stopped
    with a crash,
And the stranger turned, and his eyes they burned in a most
    peculiar way;

In a buckskin shirt that was glazed with dirt he sat, and I
    saw him sway;
Then his lips went in in a kind of grin, and he spoke, and his
    voice was calm,
And "Boys," says he, "you don't know me, and none of you
    care a damn;
But I want to state, and my words are straight, and I'll bet
    my poke they're true,
That one of you is a hound of hell . . . and that one is Dan
    McGrew."

Then I ducked my head and the lights went out, and two
    guns blazed in the dark;
And a woman screamed, and the lights went up, and two
    men lay stiff and stark.
Pitched on his head, and pumped full of lead, was
    Dangerous Dan McGrew,
While the man from the creeks lay clutched to the breast of
    the lady that's known as Lou.

These are the simple facts of the case, and I guess I ought to
   know.
They say that the stranger was crazed with "hooch," and I'm
   not denying it's so.
I'm not so wise as the lawyer guys, but strictly between us
   two—
The woman that kissed him and—pinched his poke—was
   the lady that's known as Lou.

An article in the New York Times about a Carnegie Hall tuba recital by the very real Roger Bobo was the occasion for this irresistibly joyous tribute.

RECITAL

John Updike
(1932–)

Eskimos in Manitoba,
　　Barracuda off Aruba,
Cock an ear when Roger Bobo
　　Starts to solo on the tuba.

Men of every station—Pooh-Bah,
　　Nabob, bozo, toff, and hobo—
Cry in unison, "Indubi-
　　Tably, there is simply nobo-

Dy who oompahs on the tubo,
Solo, quite like Roger Bubo!"

SPIRITUALITY

The spare beauty of Emily Dickinson's poetry only heightens the resonance of her vivid imagery. To present the concept of hope as a bird runs the risk of banality, but in this first poem the symbol seems apt and natural. The second poem may remind us that the daisy was originally called "day's eye" for its resemblance to the sun.

"HOPE" IS THE THING WITH FEATHERS

Emily Dickinson
(1830–1886)

"Hope" is the thing with feathers—
That perches in the soul—
And sings the tune without the words—
And never stops—at all—

And sweetest—in the Gale—is heard—
And sore must be the storm—
That could abash the little Bird
That kept so many warm–

I've heard it in the chillest land—
And on the strangest Sea—
Yet, never, in Extremity,
It asked a crumb—of Me.

THE DAISY FOLLOWS
SOFT THE SUN

Emily Dickinson

(1830–1886)

The daisy follows soft the sun,
And when his golden walk is done,
    Sits shyly at his feet.
He, waking, finds the flower near.
"Wherefore, marauder, art thou here?"
    "Because, sir, love is sweet!"

We are the flower, Thou the sun!
Forgive us, if as days decline,
    We nearer steal to Thee,—
Enamoured of the parting west,
The peace, the flight, the amethyst,
    Night's possibility!

Known best as the lyrics set to music by Beethoven in his Ninth Symphony, this poem is an exultant celebration of the universal spirit of brotherhood as part of a divine plan.

ODE TO JOY

Friedrich Schiller
(1759–1805)

O friends, no more these sounds!
Let us sing more cheerful songs,
More full of joy!
Joy, bright spark of divinity,
Daughter of Elysium,
Fire-inspired we tread Thy sanctuary.
Thy magic power reunites all that custom has
    divided,
All men become brothers,
Under the sway of thy gentle wings.
Whoever has created
An abiding friendship,
Or has won a true and loving wife,
All who can call at least one soul theirs,
Join our song of praise;
But those who cannot must creep tearfully
Away from our circle.
All creatures drink of joy
At nature's breast.
Just and unjust

Alike taste of her gift;
She gave us kisses and the fruit of the vine,
A true friend to the end. Even the worm can
feel contentment,
And the cherub stands before God!
Gladly, like the heavenly bodies
Which He sent on their courses
Through the splendor of the firmament;
Thus, brothers, you should run your race,
like a hero going to victory!
You millions, I embrace you.
This kiss is for all the world!
Brothers, above the starry canopy
There must dwell a loving father.
Do you fall in worship, you millions?
World, do you know your creator?
Seek Him in the heavens;
Above the stars must he dwell.

Bobby McFerrin is primarily known as an a capella jazz singer who uses his whole body for his accompaniment. In 1988 he became internationally famous for this infectious, engaging articulation of his philosophy of life.

DON'T WORRY, BE HAPPY

Bobby McFerrin
(1950–)

Here is a little song I wrote
You might want to sing it note for note
Don't worry, be happy
In every life we have some trouble
When you worry you make it double
Don't worry, be happy . . .

Ain't got no place to lay your head
Somebody came and took your bed
Don't worry, be happy
The landlord say your rent is late
He may have to litigate
Don't worry, be happy
Look at me I am happy
Don't worry, be happy
Here I give you my phone number
When you worry, call me
I make you happy
Don't worry, be happy

Ain't got no cash, ain't got no style
Ain't got no girl to make you smile
But don't worry, be happy
Cause when you worry
Your face will frown
And that will bring everybody down
So don't worry, be happy (now) . . .

There is this little song I wrote
I hope you learn it note for note
Like good little children
Don't worry, be happy
Listen to what I say
In your life expect some trouble
But when you worry
You make it double
Don't worry, be happy . . .
Don't worry don't do it, be happy
Put a smile on your face
Don't bring everybody down like this
Don't worry, it will soon pass
Whatever it is
Don't worry, be happy

The simple act of painting one's nails is an occasion to celebrate personal freedom. In the following poem the repetition of "because" in each line reminds us why such a simple act is truly uplifting, and the poem becomes a delightful litany in praise of the human spirit.

I SHALL PAINT MY NAILS RED

Carole Satyamurti

(1939–)

Because a bit of color is a public service.

Because I am proud of my hands.

Because it will remind me I'm a woman.

Because I will look like a survivor.

Because I can admire them in traffic jams.

Because my daughter will say "ugh!".

Because my lover will be surprised.

Because it is quicker than dyeing my hair.

Because it is a ten-minute moratorium.

Because it is reversible.

Published decades after the poet's death, these poems rise almost to a state of ecstasy in their celebration of the abiding transcendence of the divine within the imperfect world of humanity. Their powerful effect is enhanced by the characteristic eccentricity of Hopkins's distinctive meter and alliteration.

GOD'S GRANDEUR

Gerard Manley Hopkins
(1844–1889)

The world is charged with the grandeur of God.
It will flame out, like shining from shook foil;
It gathers to a greatness, like the ooze of oil
Crushed. Why do men then now not reck his rod?
Generations have trod, have trod, have trod;
And all is seared with trade; bleared, smeared with toil;
And wears man's smudge and shares man's smell: the soil
Is bare now, nor can foot feel, being shod.

And for all this, nature is never spent;
There lives the dearest freshness deep down things;
And though the last lights off the black West went
Oh, morning, at the brown brink eastward, springs—
Because the Holy Ghost over the bent
World broods with warm breast and with ah! bright wings.

PIED BEAUTY

Gerard Manley Hopkins
(1844–1889)

Glory be to God for dappled things—
    For skies of couple-colour as a brinded cow;
      For rose-moles all in stipple upon trout that swim;
Fresh-firecoal chestnut-falls; finches' wings;
    Landscape plotted and pieced—fold, fallow, and plough;
      And all trades, their gear and tackle and trim.

All things counter, original, spare, strange;
    Whatever is fickle, freckled (who knows how?)
      With swift, slow; sweet, sour; adazzle, dim;
He fathers-forth whose beauty is past change:
        Praise him.

The psalms attributed to King David are among the most inspirational of all religious verse. Psalm 104 may be read as a fascinating companion piece to Akhnaten's "Poem in Praise of the Sun," since it also praises the spiritual source of nature's richness and diversity (p. 34).

PSALM 104

Attributed to King David
(Reigned c. 1005–970 B.C.E.)

Bless the LORD, O my soul. O LORD my God, thou art very great; thou art clothed with honour and majesty.

Who coverest thyself with light as with a garment: who stretchest out the heavens like a curtain:

Who layeth the beams of his chambers in the waters: who maketh the clouds his chariot: who walketh upon the wings of the wind:

Who maketh his angels spirits; his ministers a flaming fire:

Who laid the foundations of the earth, that it should not be removed for ever.

Thou coveredst it with the deep as with a garment: the waters stood above the mountains.

At thy rebuke they fled; at the voice of thy thunder they
hasted away.

They go up by the mountains; they go down by the valleys
unto the place which thou hast founded for them.

Thou hast set a bound that they may not pass over; that
they turn not again to cover the earth.

He sendeth the springs into the valleys, which run among
the hills.

They give drink to every beast of the field: the wild asses
quench their thirst.

By them shall the fowls of the heaven have their habitation,
which sing among the branches.

He watereth the hills from his chambers: the earth is
satisfied with the fruit of thy works.

He causeth the grass to grow for the cattle, and herb for the
service of man: that he may bring forth food out of the
earth;

And wine that maketh glad the heart of man, and oil to
make his face to shine, and bread which strengtheneth
man's heart.

The trees of the LORD are full of sap; the cedars of
Lebanon, which he hath planted;

Where the birds make their nests: as for the stork, the fir trees are her house.

The high hills are a refuge for the wild goats; and the rocks for the conies.

He appointed the moon for seasons: the sun knoweth his going down.

Thou makest darkness, and it is night: wherein all the beasts of the forest do creep forth.

The young lions roar after their prey, and seek their meat from God.

The sun ariseth, they gather themselves together, and lay them down in their dens.

Man goeth forth unto his work and to his labour until the evening.

O LORD, how manifold are thy works! in wisdom hast thou made them all: the earth is full of thy riches.

So is this great and wide sea, wherein are things creeping innumerable, both small and great beasts.

There go the ships: there is that leviathan, whom thou hast made to play therein.

These wait all upon thee; that thou mayest give them their meat in due season.

That thou givest them they gather: thou openest thine hand, they are filled with good.

Thou hidest thy face, they are troubled: thou takest away their breath, they die, and return to their dust.

Thou sendest forth thy spirit, they are created: and thou renewest the face of the earth.

The glory of the LORD shall endure for ever: the LORD shall rejoice in his works.

He looketh on the earth, and it trembleth: he toucheth the hills, and they smoke.

I will sing unto the LORD as long as I live: I will sing praise to my GOD while I have my being.

My meditation of him shall be sweet: I will be glad in the LORD.

Let the sinners be consumed out of the earth, and let the wicked be no more. Bless thou the LORD, O my soul. Praise ye the LORD.

Among the greatest love poems in world literature is the biblical Song of Songs, attributed to King Solomon, who is said to have reigned over Israel around 3000 years ago. Although the poem's language is often picturesque and romantic, it is sometimes read as an allegorical tribute to divine love, rather than the love of a man and woman for each other. Whatever the case, the excerpt below expresses the universal joy of all people at the end of winter and the coming of the spring and the earth's rebirth. The reference to "the voice of the turtle" refers to the turtledove.

THE SONG OF SONGS

Attributed to King Solomon
(Reigned c. 970–928 B.C.E.)

My beloved spake, and said unto me,
Rise up, my love, my fair one, and come away.
For, lo, the winter is past,
the rain is over and gone;
the flowers appear on the earth;
the time of the singing of birds is come,
and the voice of the turtle is heard in our land;
the fig tree putteth forth her green figs,
and the vines with the tender grape give a good smell.
Arise, my love, my fair one, and come away.

Omar Khayyam (1048–1131) was an eminent Persian mathematician and astronomer, but his name has come down to us as the writer of the Rubaiyat *(meaning a collection of short poems with a distinctive meter and rhyme scheme). The* Rubaiyat, *in turn, is best known through Edward Fitzgerald's free translation, almost an adaptation really, that communicates in lyrical language the philosophy that though life's joys may be momentary, they are all the more precious for that reason.*

PARADISE ENOW

from the adaptation of the Rubaiyat of Omar Khayyam

Edward Fitzgerald

(1809-1883)

With me along the strip of herbage strown
That just divides the desert from the sown,
Where name of slave and sultán is forgot—
And peace to Máhmúd on his golden throne!

A book of verses underneath the bough,
A jug of wine, a loaf of bread—and Thou
Beside me singing in the wilderness—
Oh, wilderness were Paradise enow!

Some for the glories of this world; and some
Sigh for the Prophet's Paradise to come;
Ah, take the cash, and let the credit go,
Nor heed the rumble of a distant drum!

Look to the blowing Rose about us—"Lo,
Laughing," she says, "into the world I blow,
At once the silken tassel of my purse
Tear, and its treasure on the garden throw."

And those who husbanded the golden grain,
And those who flung it to the winds like rain,
Alike to no such aureate earth are turn'd
As, buried once, men want dug up again.

The worldly hope men set their hearts upon
Turns ashes—or it prospers; and anon,
Like snow upon the desert's dusty face,
Lighting a little hour or two—was gone.

Think, in this batter'd caravanserai
Whose portals are alternate Night and Day,
How Sultán after Sultán with his pomp
Abode his destin'd hour, and went his way.

They say the lion and the lizard keep
The courts where Jamshyd gloried and drank deep:
And Bahrám, that great hunter—the wild ass
Stamps o'er his head, but cannot break his sleep.

I sometimes think that never blows so red
The rose as where some buried Cæsar bled;
That every hyacinth the garden wears
Dropp'd in her lap from some once lovely head.

And this reviving herb whose tender green
Fledges the river lip on which we lean—
Ah, lean upon it lightly! for who knows
From what once lovely lip it springs unseen!

Ah, my Beloved, fill the cup that clears
To-day of past regrets and future fears:
To-morrow!—Why to-morrow I may be
Myself with Yesterday's sev'n thousand years.

For some we lov'd, the loveliest and the best
That from his vintage rolling Time has prest,
Have drunk their cup a round or two before,
And one by one crept silently to rest.

And we, that now make merry in the room
They left, and Summer dresses in new bloom,
Ourselves must we beneath the couch of earth
Descend—ourselves to make a couch—for whom?

Ah, make the most of what we yet may spend,
Before we too into the dust descend;
Dust into dust, and under dust, to lie,
Sans wine, sans song, sans singer, and—sans end!

The subtitle of the first poem below is "What the Heart of the Young Man said to the Psalmist," but the concept of dust's returning to dust originates not in the Psalms, but in Genesis 3:19: "for dust thou art, and unto dust shalt thou return"; in the Anglican Book of Common Prayer, the burial service reads in part "we . . . commit his body to the ground; earth to earth; ashes to ashes, dust to dust." Of course Longfellow's point is that the human soul transcends the death of the body, and that we should not think of life as vainly leading to nothing, but as offering an opportunity to improve the world for others who come after us. The second poem here celebrates the poet's love for the river that flows near his home (the Charles River divides Cambridge, Massachusetts, from Boston), a river that recalls to him the flow of his own life, consoling and inspiring him through moments both of sadness and of joy.

A PSALM OF LIFE

Henry Wadsworth Longfellow
(1807–1882)

Tell me not in mournful numbers,
"Life is but an empty dream!"
For the soul is dead that slumbers,
And things are not what they seem.

Life is real! Life is earnest!
And the grave is not its goal;
"Dust thou art, to dust returnest,"
Was not spoken of the soul.

Not enjoyment, and not sorrow,
Is our destined end or way;
But to act, that each to-morrow
Find us further than to-day.

Art is long, and Time is fleeting,
And our hearts, though stout and brave,
Still, like muffled drums, are beating
Funeral marches to the grave.

In the world's broad field of battle,
In the bivouac of Life,
Be not like dumb, driven cattle!
Be a hero in the strife!

Trust no Future, howe'er pleasant!
Let the dead Past bury its dead!
Act—act in the living Present!
Heart within, and God o'erhead!

Lives of great men all remind us
We can make our lives sublime,
And, departing, leave behind us
Footprints on the sands of time;

Footprints, that perhaps another,
Sailing o'er life's solemn main,
A forlorn and shipwrecked brother,
Seeing, shall take heart again.

Let us, then, be up and doing,
With a heart for any fate;
Still achieving, still pursuing,
Learn to labor and to wait.

TO THE RIVER CHARLES

Henry Wadsworth Longfellow

(1807–1882)

River! that in silence windest
   Through the meadows, bright and free,
Till at length thy rest thou findest
   In the bosom of the sea!

Four long years of mingled feeling,
   Half in rest, and half in strife,
I have seen thy waters stealing
   Onward, like the stream of life.

Thou hast taught me, Silent River!
   Many a lesson, deep and long;
Thou hast been a generous giver;
   I can give thee but a song.

Oft in sadness and in illness,
   I have watched thy current glide,
Till the beauty of its stillness
   Overflowed me, like a tide.

And in better hours and brighter,
   When I saw thy waters gleam,
I have felt my heart beat lighter,
   And leap onward with thy stream.

Not for this alone I love thee,
　　Nor because thy waves of blue
From celestial seas above thee
　　Take their own celestial hue.

Where yon shadowy woodlands hide thee,
　　And thy waters disappear,
Friends I love have dwelt beside thee,
　　And have made thy margin dear.

More than this;—thy name reminds me
　　Of three friends, all true and tried;
And that name, like magic, binds me
　　Closer, closer to thy side.

Friends my soul with joy remembers!
　　How like quivering flames they start,
When I fan the living embers
　　On the hearth-stone of my heart!

'T is for this, thou Silent River!
　　That my spirit leans to thee;
Thou hast been a generous giver,
　　Take this idle song from me.

Gilbert Keith Chesterton converted to Catholicism when he was in middle age, and espoused his faith with passion and pictur-esque language. This poem presents the story of Christ's entrance into Jerusalem on the back of a donkey from the point of view of a creature whose entire existence is validated by one transcendent moment.

THE DONKEY

G. K. Chesterton
(1874–1936)

When fishes flew and forests walked,
    And figs grew upon thorn,
Some moment when the moon was blood,
    Then surely I was born;

With monstrous head and sickening cry
    And ears like errant wings,
The devil's walking parody
    Of all four-footed things.

The tattered outlaw of the earth,
    Of ancient crooked will;
Starve, scourge, deride me: I am dumb,
    I keep my secret still.

Fools! For I also had my hour;
    One far fierce hour and sweet;
There was a shout about my ears,
    And palms before my feet.

The title of this familiar and inspiring hymn derives from the Nicene Creed ("I believe in one God, the Father Almighty, maker of heaven and earth, and of all things visible and invisible"), and the term can be traced back even further to Psalms 146:6 ("the Maker of heaven and earth, the sea, and everything in them—the LORD, who remains faithful forever"). In recent years, the first verse has become perhaps better known for providing the titles to the classic novels by James Herriot based on his life as a veterinarian in Yorkshire in the 1940s.

MAKER OF HEAVEN AND EARTH
(ALL THINGS BRIGHT
AND BEAUTIFUL)

Cecil Frances Alexander
(1818–1895)

All things bright and beautiful,
All creatures great and small,
All things wise and wonderful,
The Lord God made them all.

Each little flower that opens,
Each little bird that sings,
He made their glowing colours,
He made their tiny wings.

The rich man in his castle,
The poor man at his gate,

God made them, high or lowly,
And ordered their estate.

The purple-headed mountain,
The river running by,
The sunset, and the morning,
That brightens up the sky;

The cold wind in the winter,
The pleasant summer sun,
The ripe fruits in the garden,
He made them every one.

The tall trees in the greenwood,
The meadows where we play,
The rushes by the water,
We gather every day;

He gave us eyes to see them,
And lips that we might tell,
How great is God Almighty,
Who has made all things well.

Leigh Hunt was a close friend of many notable nineteenth-century British literary figures, including Shelley, Keats, Byron, and Thomas Carlyle. Both of the following poems involve a visiting angel. The first poem is based upon a Sufi legend recorded by the Persian mystic and poet Rumi. The second contrasts the visit of an imaginary angel with the presence of those closest to us who are in effect "angels that are to be."

ABOU BEN ADHEM

Leigh Hunt
(1784–1859)

Abou Ben Adhem (may his tribe increase)
Awoke one night from a deep dream of peace,
And saw—within the moonlight in his room,
Making it rich, and like a lily in bloom—
An angel, writing in a book of gold.
Exceeding peace had made Ben Adhem bold,
And to the presence in the room he said,
"What writest thou?" The vision raised its head,
And, with a look made of all sweet accord,
Answered, "The names of those who love the Lord."
"And is mine one?" said Abou. "Nay, not so,"
Replied the angel. Abou spoke more low,
But cheerly still, and said, "I pray thee, then,
Write me as one that loves his fellow men."
The angel wrote, and vanish'd. The next night
It came again with a great wakening light,
And show'd the names whom love of God had blessed,
And lo! Ben Adhem's name led all the rest.

AN ANGEL IN THE HOUSE

Leigh Hunt

(1784–1859)

How sweet it were, if without feeble fright,
Or dying of the dreadful beauteous sight,
An angel came to us, and we could bear
To see him issue from the silent air
At evening in our room, and bend on ours
His divine eyes, and bring us from his bowers
News of dear friends, and children who have never
Been dead indeed, as we shall know forever.
Alas! we think not what we daily see
About our hearths, angels that are to be,
Or may be if they will, and we prepare
Their souls and ours to meet in happy air;—
A child, a friend, a wife whose soft heart sings
In unison with ours, breeding its future wings.

Among the sketchy details known about Thomas Dekker's life, the most prominent is that he lived in almost constant poverty and spent time in debtors' prison. Yet judging from the following poem he seems to have found a sense of satisfaction in what are normally called the simple things of life, and especially in the sheer pleasure of honest toil. The "hey nonny nonny" refrain is often found in Elizabethan lyrics, including those of Shakespeare.

SWEET CONTENT

Thomas Dekker

(1572–1632)

Art thou poor, yet hast thou golden slumbers?
    O sweet content!
Art thou rich, yet is thy mind perplex'd?
    O punishment!
To add to golden numbers golden numbers?
    O sweet content! O sweet, O sweet content!
Work apace, apace, apace, apace;
Honest labour bears a lovely face;
Then hey nonny nonny—hey nonny nonny!

Canst drink the waters of the crispèd spring?
    O sweet content!
Swim'st thou in wealth, yet sink'st in thine own tears?
    O punishment!
Then he that patiently want's burden bears,

No burden bears, but is a king, a king!
O sweet content! O sweet, O sweet content!
Work apace, apace, apace, apace;
Honest labour bears a lovely face;
Then hey nonny nonny—hey nonny nonny!

Blake was a mystical and lyrical poet who wrote poems featuring the contrasting states of the human soul in Songs of Innocence *and* Songs of Experience. *The latter is typified by his famous poem "The Tyger," while in the first of the following poems the poet celebrates the childlike purity of the lamb as a reflection of divine love. The second poem here is a pure expression of the simple joys of childhood itself, which seems to share its laughter with the natural world around us.*

THE LAMB

William Blake

(1757–1827)

Little lamb, who made thee?
Dost thou know who made thee?
Gave thee life, and bid thee feed,
By the stream and o'er the mead;
Gave thee clothing of delight,
Softest clothing, wooly, bright;
Gave thee such a tender voice,
Making all the vales rejoice?
Little lamb, who made thee?
Dost thou know who made thee?

Little lamb, I'll tell thee,
Little lamb, I'll tell thee:
He is callèd by thy name,
For He calls Himself a Lamb.
He is meek, and He is mild;

He became a little child.
I a child, and thou a lamb,
We are callèd by His name.
Little lamb, God bless thee!
Little lamb, God bless thee!

LAUGHING SONG

William Blake

(1757–1827)

When the green woods laugh with the voice of joy,
And the dimpling stream runs laughing by;
When the air does laugh with our merry wit,
And the green hill laughs with the noise of it;

When the meadows laugh with lively green,
And the grasshopper laughs in the merry scene;
When Mary and Susan and Emily,
With their sweet round mouths sing "Ha, ha, he!"

When the painted birds laugh in the shade,
Where our table with cherries and nuts is spread:
Come live, and be merry and join with me,
To sing the sweet chorus of "Ha, ha, he!"

Here are two very different poems on death that are surprisingly comforting and even inspiring. Written when its author was seventeen years old, "Thanatopsis" (the title means "view of death") is both a great poem of consolation and a majestic meditation on humankind's intimate relationship with the rest of nature. In "Death Be Not Proud" the great English cleric-poet John Donne mocks the idea of Death, and even threatens it with its own extinction.

THANATOPSIS

William Cullen Bryant
(1794–1878)

To him who in the love of Nature holds
Communion with her visible forms, she speaks
A various language; for his gayer hours
She has a voice of gladness, and a smile
And eloquence of beauty, and she glides
Into his darker musings, with a mild
And healing sympathy, that steals away
Their sharpness, ere he is aware. When thoughts
Of the last bitter hour come like a blight
Over thy spirit, and sad images
Of the stern agony, and shroud, and pall,
And breathless darkness, and the narrow house,
Make thee to shudder, and grow sick at heart;—
Go forth under the open sky, and list
To Nature's teachings, while from all around—
Earth and her waters, and the depths of air—

Comes a still voice—Yet a few days, and thee
The all-beholding sun shall see no more
In all his course; nor yet in the cold ground,
Where thy pale form was laid, with many tears,
Nor in the embrace of ocean, shall exist
Thy image. Earth, that nourished thee, shall claim
Thy growth, to be resolved to earth again,
And, lost each human trace, surrendering up
Thine individual being, shalt thou go
To mix forever with the elements,
To be a brother to the insensible rock,
And to the sluggish clod, which the rude swain
Turns with his share, and treads upon. The oak
Shall send his roots abroad, and pierce thy mould.

Yet not to thine eternal resting-place
Shalt thou retire alone, nor couldst thou wish
Couch more magnificent. Thou shalt lie down
With patriarchs of the infant world,—with kings,
The powerful of the earth,—the wise, the good,
Fair forms, and hoary seers of ages past,
All in one mighty sepulchre. The hills
Rock-ribbed and ancient as the sun,—the vales
Stretching in pensive quietness between;
The venerable woods—rivers that move
In majesty, and the complaining brooks
That make the meadows green; and, poured round all,
Old Ocean's gray and melancholy waste,—
Are but the solemn decorations all
Of the great tomb of man. The golden sun,
The planets, all the infinite host of heaven,

Are shining on the sad abodes of death,
Through the still lapse of ages. All that tread
The globe are but a handful to the tribes
That slumber in its bosom.—Take the wings
Of morning, pierce the Barcan wilderness,
Or lose thyself in the continuous woods
Where rolls the Oregon, and hears no sound,
Save his own dashings,—yet the dead are there:
And millions in those solitudes, since first
The flight of years began, have laid them down
In their last sleep—the dead reign there alone.
So shalt thou rest, and what if thou withdraw
In silence from the living, and no friend
Take note of thy departure? All that breathe
Will share thy destiny. The gay will laugh
When thou art gone, the solemn brood of care
Plod on, and each one as before will chase
His favorite phantom; yet all these shall leave
Their mirth and their employments, and shall come
And make their bed with thee. As the long train
Of ages glide away, the sons of men,
The youth in life's green spring, and he who goes
In the full strength of years, matron and maid,
The speechless babe, and the gray-headed man—
Shall one by one be gathered to thy side,
By those, who in their turn shall follow them.

So live, that when thy summons comes to join
The innumerable caravan, which moves
To that mysterious realm, where each shall take
His chamber in the silent halls of death,

Thou go not, like the quarry-slave at night,
Scourged to his dungeon, but, sustained and soothed
By an unfaltering trust, approach thy grave
Like one who wraps the drapery of his couch
About him, and lies down to pleasant dreams.

DEATH BE NOT PROUD

John Donne

(1572–1631)

Death be not proud, though some have called thee
Mighty and dreadfull, for, thou art not so,
For, those, whom thou think'st, thou dost overthrow,
Die not, poore death, nor yet canst thou kill me.
From rest and sleepe, which but thy pictures bee,
Much pleasure, then from thee, much more must flow,
And soonest our best men with thee doe goe,
Rest of their bones, and soules deliverie.
Thou art slave to Fate, Chance, kings, and desperate men,
And dost with poyson, warre, and sicknesse dwell,
And poppie, or charmes can make us sleepe as well,
And better then thy stroake; why swell'st thou then;
One short sleepe past, wee wake eternally,
And death shall be no more; death, thou shalt die.

George Herbert was notable for his piety and the power of his verses. In the first of these strongly symbolic poems, he seems to say that peace may be found not in the material things of this world, but in the "secret virtue" of leading a good life. In the second, the poet identifies himself with a flower that blooms and then dies with the frost only to flower again in the coming year, awaiting God's paradise where an eternal garden awaits.

PEACE

George Herbert

(1593–1633)

Sweet Peace, where dost thou dwell? I humbly crave,
Let me once know.
I sought thee in a secret cave,
And ask'd, if Peace were there,
A hollow wind did seem to answer, No:
Go seek elsewhere.

I did; and going did a rainbow note:
Surely, thought I,
This is the lace of Peace's coat:
I will search out the matter.
But while I looked the clouds immediately
Did break and scatter.

Then went I to a garden and did spy
A gallant flower,
The crown-imperial: Sure, said I,

Peace at the root must dwell.
But when I digged, I saw a worm devour
What showed so well.

At length I met a rev'rend good old man;
Whom when for Peace

I did demand, he thus began:
There was a Prince of old
At Salem dwelt, who lived with good increase
Of flock and fold.

He sweetly lived; yet sweetness did not save
His life from foes.
But after death out of his grave
There sprang twelve stalks of wheat;
Which many wond'ring at, got some of those
To plant and set.

It prospered strangely, and did soon disperse
Through all the earth:
For they that taste it do rehearse
That virtue lies therein;
A secret virtue, bringing peace and mirth
By flight of sin.

Take of this grain, which in my garden grows,
And grows for you;
Make bread of it: and that repose
And peace, which ev'ry where
With so much earnestness you do pursue,
Is only there.

THE FLOWER

George Herbert

(1593–1633)

How Fresh, O Lord, how sweet and clean
Are thy returns! ev'n as the flowers in spring;
To which, besides their own demean,
The late-past frosts tributes of pleasure bring.
Grief melts away
Like snow in May,
As if there were no such cold thing.

Who would have thought my shrivel'd heart
Could have recover'd greennesse? It was gone
Quite under ground; as flowers depart
To see their mother-root, when they have blown;
Where they together
All the hard weather,
Dead to the world, keep house unknown.

These are thy wonders, Lord of power,
Killing and quickning, bringing down to hell
And up to heaven in an houre;
Making a chiming of a passing-bell,
We say amisse,
This or that is:
Thy word is all, if we could spell.

O that I once past changing were;
Fast in thy Paradise, where no flower can wither!

Many a spring I shoot up fair,
Offring at heav'n, growing and groning thither:
Nor doth my flower
Want a spring-showre,
My sinnes and I joining together;

But while I grow to a straight line;
Still upwards bent, as if heav'n were mine own,
Thy anger comes, and I decline:
What frost to that? what pole is not the zone,
Where all things burn,
When thou dost turn,
And the least frown of thine is shown?

And now in age I bud again,
After so many deaths I live and write;
I once more smell the dew and rain,
And relish versing: O my onely light,
It cannot be
That I am he
On whom thy tempests fell all night.

These are thy wonders, Lord of love,
To make us see we are but flowers that glide:
Which when we once can finde and prove,
Thou hast a garden for us, where to bide.
Who would be more,
Swelling through store,
Forfeit their Paradise by their pride.

When Henley wrote of the indomitability of the human spirit, he wrote from his own experience. He suffered all his life from a painful bone disease that resulted in the amputation of one of his feet, but he was still able to graduate from Oxford with honors and go on to a notable career as a writer. The title of the poem is the Latin word for "unconquered."

INVICTUS

William Ernest Henley
(1849–1903)

Out of the night that covers me,
 Black as the Pit from pole to pole,
I thank whatever gods may be
 For my unconquerable soul.

In the fell clutch of circumstance
 I have not winced nor cried aloud.
Under the bludgeonings of chance
 My head is bloody, but unbowed.

Beyond this place of wrath and tears
 Looms but the Horror of the shade,
And yet the menace of the years
 Finds, and shall find, me unafraid.

It matters not how strait the gate,
 How charged with punishments the scroll,
I am the master of my fate;
 I am the captain of my soul.

Perhaps no poem in the English language contains such sheer propulsive power as this one. The words hold within them the sounds they describe, and to recite this poem aloud is to forget one's troubles and be carried away into a virtual ecstatic state— "bells, bells, bells, bells, bells, bells, bells"!

THE BELLS

Edgar Allan Poe
(1809–1849)

I

Hear the sledges with the bells—
Silver bells!
What a world of merriment their melody foretells!
How they tinkle, tinkle, tinkle,
In the icy air of night!
While the stars that oversprinkle
All the heavens seem to twinkle
With a crystalline delight;
Keeping time, time, time,
In a sort of Runic rhyme,
To the tintinnabulation that so musically wells
From the bells, bells, bells, bells,
Bells, bells, bells—
From the jingling and the tinkling of the bells.

II

Hear the mellow wedding bells—
Golden bells!

What a world of happiness their harmony foretells!
Through the balmy air of night
How they ring out their delight!
From the molten-golden notes,
And all in tune,
What a liquid ditty floats
To the turtle-dove that listens, while she gloats
On the moon!
Oh, from out the sounding cells
What a gush of euphony voluminously wells!
How it swells!
How it dwells
On the Future!—how it tells
Of the rapture that impels
To the swinging and the ringing
Of the bells, bells, bells,
Of the bells, bells, bells, bells,
Bells, bells, bells—
To the rhyming and the chiming of the bells!

III

Hear the loud alarum bells—
Brazen bells!
What a tale of terror, now, their turbulency tells!
In the startled ear of night
How they scream out their affright!
Too much horrified to speak,
They can only shriek, shriek,
Out of tune,
In a clamorous appealing to the mercy of the fire,
In a mad expostulation with the deaf and frantic fire,
Leaping higher, higher, higher,

With a desperate desire,
And a resolute endeavor
Now—now to sit or never,
By the side of the pale-faced moon.
Oh, the bells, bells, bells!
What a tale their terror tells
Of despair!
How they clang, and clash, and roar!
What a horror they outpour
On the bosom of the palpitating air!
Yet the ear it fully knows,
By the twanging
And the clanging,
How the danger ebbs and flows;
Yet the ear distinctly tells,
In the jangling
And the wrangling,
How the danger sinks and swells,
By the sinking or the swelling in the anger of the bells—
Of the bells,
Of the bells, bells, bells, bells,
Bells, bells, bells—
In the clamor and the clangor of the bells!

IV

Hear the tolling of the bells—
Iron bells!
What a world of solemn thought their monody compels!
In the silence of the night,
How we shiver with affright
At the melancholy menace of their tone!
For every sound that floats

From the rust within their throats
Is a groan.
And the people—ah, the people—
They that dwell up in the steeple,
All alone,
And who tolling, tolling, tolling,
In that muffled monotone,
Feel a glory in so rolling
On the human heart a stone—
They are neither man nor woman—
They are neither brute nor human—
They are Ghouls:
And their king it is who tolls;
And he rolls, rolls, rolls,
Rolls
A paean from the bells!
And his merry bosom swells
With the paean of the bells!
And he dances, and he yells;
Keeping time, time, time,
In a sort of Runic rhyme,
To the paean of the bells,
Of the bells—
Keeping time, time, time,
In a sort of Runic rhyme,
To the throbbing of the bells,
Of the bells, bells, bells—
To the sobbing of the bells;
Keeping time, time, time,
As he knells, knells, knells,
In a happy Runic rhyme,

To the rolling of the bells,
Of the bells, bells, bells—
To the tolling of the bells,
Of the bells, bells, bells, bells,
Bells, bells, bells—
To the moaning and the groaning of the bells.

Thomas Traherne believed that divine beauty could be found in a child's perspective and his poetry is often told from the inno-cent viewpoint of youth. In the following poem, a newborn baby is awe-inspired by its first impressions of the world.

WONDER

Thomas Traherne

(1636–1674)

How like an Angel came I down!
How bright are all things here!
When first among His works I did appear
O how their glory me did crown!
The world resembled His Eternity,
In which my soul did walk;
And every thing that I did see
Did with me talk.

The skies in their magnificence,
The lively, lovely air,
Oh how divine, how soft, how sweet, how fair!
The stars did entertain my sense,
And all the works of God, so bright and pure,
So rich and great did seem,
As if they ever must endure
In my esteem.

A native health and innocence
Within my bones did grow,

And while my God did all his Glories show,
   I felt a vigour in my sense
That was all Spirit. I within did flow
    With seas of life, like wine;
   I nothing in the world did know
     But 'twas divine.

   Harsh ragged objects were concealed,
    Oppressions, tears and cries,
Sins, griefs, complaints, dissensions, weeping eyes
   Were hid, and only things revealed
Which heavenly Spirits and the Angels prize.
    The state of Innocence
   And bliss, not trades and poverties,
     Did fill my sense.

   The streets were paved with golden stones,
    The boys and girls were mine,
Oh how did all their lovely faces shine!
   The sons of men were holy ones,
In joy and beauty they appeared to me,
    And every thing which here I found,
   While like an Angel I did see,
     Adorned the ground.

   Rich diamond and pearl and gold
    In every place was seen;
Rare splendours, yellow, blue, red, white and green,
   Mine eyes did everywhere behold.
Great wonders clothed with glory did appear,
    Amazement was my bliss,

That and my wealth was everywhere;
　　No joy to this!

Cursed and devised proprieties,
　　With envy, avarice
And fraud, those fiends that spoil even Paradise,
　　Flew from the splendour of mine eyes,
And so did hedges, ditches, limits, bounds,
　　I dreamed not aught of those,
　　But wandered over all men's grounds,
　　　　And found repose.

Proprieties themselves were mine,
　　And hedges ornaments;
Walls, boxes, coffers, and their rich contents
　　Did not divide my joys, but all combine.
Clothes, ribbons, jewels, laces, I esteemed
　　My joys by others worn:
　　For me they all to wear them seemed
　　　　When I was born.

Christina Rosetti was a devout Catholic and her poetry reflects her ardent faith. The repeating lines in each stanza of "A Hope Carol" seem to invoke the divine spirit, like reciting a prayer. The second poem here is a parable of salvation, as a long and arduous journey ends in the comfort of an inn.

A HOPE CAROL

Christina Rossetti
(1830–1894)

A night was near, a day was near,
Between a day and night
I heard sweet voices calling clear,
Calling me:
I heard a whirr of wing on wing,
But could not see the sight;
I long to see my birds that sing,—
I long to see.

Below the stars, beyond the moon,
Between the night and day,
I heard a rising falling tune
Calling me:
I long to see the pipes and strings
Whereon such minstrels play;
I long to see each face that sings,—
I long to see.
To-day or may be not to-day,
To-night or not to-night;

All voices that command or pray
Calling me,
Shall kindle in my soul such fire,
And in my eyes such light,
That I shall see that heart's desire
I long to see.

UP-HILL

Christina Rossetti
(1830–1894)

Does the road wind up-hill all the way?
    Yes, to the very end.
Will the day's journey take the whole long day?
    From morn to night, my friend.

But is there for the night a resting-place?
    A roof for when the slow dark hours begin.
May not the darkness hide it from my face?
    You cannot miss that inn.

Shall I meet other wayfarers at night?
    Those who have gone before.
Then must I knock, or call when just in sight?
    They will not keep you standing at that door.

Shall I find comfort, travel-sore and weak?
    Of labor you shall find the sum.
Will there be beds for me and all who seek?
    Yea, beds for all who come.

Copies of "Desiderata" were widely circulated in poster form in the 1960s, and attributed to a work from the seventeenth century believed to have been found in an old churchyard. Actually the poem was written much later by a lawyer and sometime poet from Indiana. It was later included in a collection of inspirational writings by the rector of St. Paul's Church in Baltimore, leading to the mistaken assumption that it was anonymous and centuries old. But whatever its origin, its quiet message continues to resonate and inspire. The second poem here is less familiar, but emerges from the same humane spirit as the first, and even evokes sentiments reminiscent of the Beatitudes of Jesus.

DESIDERATA

Max Ehrmann
(1872–1945)

Go placidly amid the noise and haste,
and remember what peace there may be in silence.
As far as possible, without surrender,
be on good terms with all persons.
Speak your truth quietly and clearly;
and listen to others,
even to the dull and ignorant; they
too have their story.

Avoid loud and aggressive persons,
they are vexations to the spirit.
If you compare yourself with others,
you may become vain and bitter,

for always there will be greater and lesser persons than
    yourself.
Enjoy your achievements as well as your plans.

Keep interested in your own career, however humble;
it is a real possession in the changing fortunes of time.
Exercise caution in your business affairs,
for the world is full of trickery.
But let this not blind you to what virtue there is;
many persons strive for high ideals,
and everywhere life is full of heroism.

Be yourself.
Especially do not feign affection.
Neither be cynical about love;
for in the face of all aridity and disenchantment
it is as perennial as the grass.

Take kindly the counsel of the years,
gracefully surrendering the things of youth.
Nurture strength of spirit to shield you in sudden
    misfortune.
But do not distress yourself with dark imaginings.
Many fears are born of fatigue and loneliness.
Beyond a wholesome discipline,
be gentle with yourself.

You are a child of the universe
no less than the trees and the stars;
you have a right to be here.
And whether or not it is clear to you,
no doubt the universe is unfolding as it should.

Therefore be at peace with God,
whatever you conceive Him to be.
And whatever your labors and aspirations,
in the noisy confusion of life, keep peace with your soul.

With all its sham, drudgery and broken dreams,
it is still a beautiful world.
Be cheerful. Strive to be happy.

A PRAYER

Max Ehrmann
(1872–1945)

Let me do my work each day; and if the
darkened hours of despair
overcome me, may I not forget the strength
that comforted me
in the desolation of other times.

May I still remember the bright hours that
found me walking over
the silent hills of my childhood, or dreaming
on the margin of a quiet
river, when a light glowed within me, and
I promised my early God
to have courage amid the tempests of the
changing years.

Spare me from bitterness and from the
sharp passions of unguarded
moments. May I not forget that poverty and
riches are of the spirit.
Though the world knows me not, may my
thoughts and actions be
such as shall keep me friendly with myself.

Lift up my eyes from the earth, and let me not
forget the uses of the
stars. Forbid that I should judge others lest
I condemn myself.
Let me not follow the clamor of the world,
but walk calmly in my
path.

Give me a few friends who will love me for what
I am; and keep ever
burning before my vagrant steps the kindly
light of hope.

And though age and infirmity overtake me,
and I come not within
sight of the castle of my dreams, teach me
still to be thankful for
life, and for time's olden memories that are good
and sweet; and
may the evening's twilight find me gentle still.

THE HUMAN
CONNECTION

The identity of the guest Ben Jonson had in mind when he wrote this poem is unknown, and perhaps it was no one. His apparently humble invitation becomes increasingly outrageous and ironic with each new delicacy that will be served at the lavish feast.

INVITING A FRIEND TO SUPPER

Ben Jonson
(1572–1637)

Tonight, grave sir, both my poor house and I
Do equally desire your company;
Not that we think us worthy such a guest,
But that your worth will dignify our feast
With those that come; whose grace may make that seem
Something, which else could hope for no esteem.
It is the fair acceptance, sir, creates
The entertainment perfect, not the cates.
Yet you shall have, to rectify your palate,
An olive, capers, or some better salad
Ushering the mutton; with a short-legged hen,
If we can get her, full of eggs, and then
Lemons, and wine for sauce; to these, a coney
Is not to be despaired of, for our money;
And though fowl now be scarce, yet there are clerks,
The sky not falling, think we may have larks.
I'll tell you of more, and lie, so you will come:
Of partridge, pheasant, woodcock, of which some
May yet be there; and godwit, if we can;
Knat, rail and ruff, too. Howsoe'er, my man

Shall read a piece of Virgil, Tacitus,
Livy, or of some better book to us,
Of which we'll speak our minds, amidst our meat;
And I'll profess no verses to repeat;
To this, if aught appear which I not know of,
That will the pastry, not my paper, show of.
Digestive cheese and fruit there sure will be;
But that which most doth take my muse and me
Is a pure cup of rich Canary wine,
Which is the Mermaid's now, but shall be mine;
Of which had Horace or Anacreon tasted,
Their lives, as do their lines, till now had lasted.
Tobacco, nectar, or the Thespian spring
Are all but Luther's beer to this I sing.
Of this we will sup free, but moderately;
And we will have no Poley or Parrot by;
Nor shall our cups make any guilty men,
But at our parting we will be as when
We innocently met. No simple word
That shall be uttered at our mirthful board
Shall make us sad next morning, or affright
The liberty that we'll enjoy tonight.

This outrageous ballad about a bowl of soup prompts a smile every time the word "bouillabaisse" is read aloud. As the poem switches from English to French, it proves to be quite a mouthful, but just as Thackeray writes of returning to the inn to reminisce about eating that marvelous dish in the company of good friends, one can't resist reading this ballad again and again.

THE BALLAD OF BOUILLABAISSE

W. M. Thackeray

(1811–1863)

A street there is in Paris famous,
For which no rhyme our language yields,
Rue Neuve des Petits Champs its name is—
The New Street of the Little Fields;
And there's an inn, not rich and splendid,
But still in comfortable case;
The which in youth I oft attended,
To eat a bowl of Bouillabaisse.

This Bouillabaisse a noble dish is—
A sort of soup or broth, or brew,
Or hotchpotch, of all sorts of fishes,
That Greenwich never could outdo;
Green herbs, red peppers, mussels, saffern,
Soles, onions, garlic, roach, and dace;
All these you eat at Terré's tavern,
In that one dish of Bouillabaisse.

Indeed, a rich and savoury stew 'tis;
And true philosophers, methinks,
Who love all sorts of natural beauties,
Should love good victuals and good drinks.
And Cordelier or Benedictine
Might gladly, sure, his lot embrace,
Nor find a fast-day too afflicting
Which served him up a Bouillabaisse.

I wonder if the house still there is?
Yes, here the lamp is, as before;
The smiling, red-cheek'd écaillère is
Still opening oysters at the door.
Is Terré still alive and able?
I recollect his droll grimace;
He'd come and smile before your table,
And hope you liked your Bouillabaisse.

We enter—nothing's changed or older.
"How's Monsieur Terré, waiter, pray?"
The waiter stares and shrugs his shoulder—
"Monsieur is dead this many a day."
"It is the lot of saint and sinner,
So honest Terré's run his race!"
"What will Monsieur require for dinner?"
"Say, do you still cook Bouillabaisse?"

"Oh, oui, Monsieur," 's the waiter's answer;
"Quel vin Monsieur désire-t-il?"
"Tell me a good one."—"That I can, Sir:
The Chambertin with yellow seal."
"So Terré's gone," I say, and sink in

My old accustom'd corner-place;
"He's done with feasting and with drinking,
With Burgundy and Bouillabaisse."

My old accustom'd corner here is,
The table still is in the nook;
Ah! vanish'd many a busy year is,
This well-known chair since last I took.
When first I saw ye, *cari luoghi*,
I'd scarce a beard upon my face,
And now a grizzled, grim old fogy,
I sit and wait for Bouillabaisse.

Where are you, old companions trusty,
Of early days, here met to dine?
Come, waiter! quick, a flagon crusty—
I'll pledge them in the good old wine.
The kind old voices and old faces
My memory can quick retrace;
Around the board they take their places,
And share the wine and Bouillabaisse.

There's Jack has made a wondrous marriage;
There's laughing Tom is laughing yet;
There's brave Augustus drives his carriage;
There's poor old Fred in the Gazette;
On James's head the grass is growing:
Good Lord! the world has wagged apace
Since here we set the Claret flowing,
And drank, and ate the Bouillabaisse.

Ah me! how quick the days are flitting!
I mind me of a time that's gone,
When here I'd sit, as now I'm sitting,
In this same place—but not alone.
A fair young form was nestled near me,
A dear, dear face looked fondly up,
And sweetly spoke and smiled to cheer me
—There's no one now to share my cup.

I drink it as the Fates ordain it.
Come, fill it, and have done with rhymes:
Fill up the lonely glass, and drain it
In memory of dear old times.
Welcome the wine, whate'er the seal is;
And sit you down and say your grace
With thankful heart, whate'er the meal is.
—Here comes the smoking Bouillabaisse!

The epigraph to the first poem here is from The Iliad, an indication that the poet's sentiments are not original, but are imbedded in our culture. It indicates that to be remembered not so much for great deeds but for being kind to one's fellow man is a not insignificant accomplishment. The second poem is written in a rather exaggerated and folksy dialect, but its central message is essentially the same as that of the biblical tale of the Good Samaritan: we are all each other's neighbors.

THE HOUSE BY THE SIDE OF THE ROAD

Sam Walter Foss
(1858–1911)

> *"He was a friend to man, and lived*
> *In a house by the side of the road."*
> —Homer

There are hermit souls that live withdrawn
In the place of their self-content;
There are souls like stars, that dwell apart,
In a fellowless firmament;
There are pioneer souls that blaze the paths
Where highways never ran—
But let me live by the side of the road
And be a friend to man.

Let me live in a house by the side of the road
Where the race of men go by—
The men who are good and the men who are bad,
As good and as bad as I.
I would not sit in the scorner's seat
Nor hurl the cynic's ban—
Let me live in a house by the side of the road
And be a friend to man.

I see from my house by the side of the road
By the side of the highway of life,
The men who press with the ardor of hope,
The men who are faint with the strife,
But I turn not away from their smiles and tears,
Both parts of an infinite plan—
Let me live in a house by the side of the road
And be a friend to man.

I know there are brook-gladdened meadows ahead,
And mountains of wearisome height;
That the road passes on through the long afternoon
And stretches away to the night.
And still I rejoice when the travelers rejoice
And weep with the strangers that moan,
Nor live in my house by the side of the road
Like a man who dwells alone.

Let me live in my house by the side of the road,
Where the race of men go by—
They are good, they are bad, they are weak, they are strong,
Wise, foolish—so am I.

Then why should I sit in the scorner's seat,
Or hurl the cynic's ban?
Let me live in my house by the side of the road
And be a friend to man.

HULLO

Sam Walter Foss
(1858–1911)

W'en you see a man in woe,
Walk right up and say "Hullo!"
Say "Hullo" and "How d'ye do?
How's the world a-usin' you?"
Slap the fellow on the back;
Bring your hand down with a whack;
Walk right up, and don't go slow;
Grin an' shake, an' say "Hullo!"

Is he clothed in rags? Oh! sho;
Walk right up an' say "Hullo!"
Rags is but a cotton roll
Jest for wrappin' up a soul;
An' a soul is worth a true
Hale and hearty "How d'ye do?"
Don't wait for the crowd to go,
Walk right up and say "Hullo!"

When big vessels meet, they say
They saloot an' sail away.
Jest the same are you an' me
Lonesome ships upon a sea;
Each one sailin' his own log,
For a port behind the fog;
Let your speakin' trumpet blow;
Lift your horn an' cry "Hullo!"

Say "Hullo!" an' "How d'ye do?"
Other folks are good as you.
W'en you leave your house of clay
Wanderin' in the far away,
W'en you travel through the strange
Country t'other side the range,
Then the souls you've cheered will know
Who ye be, an' say "Hullo."

Edgar Guest was known as "the poet of the people," because he valued everyday life in his poetry. Guest captures the warmth of a home with familiar language and optimistic themes in the following poems.

HOME

Edgar Guest
(1881–1959)

It takes a heap o' livin' in a house t' make it home,
A heap o' sun an' shadder, an' ye sometimes have t' roam
Afore ye really 'preciate the things ye lef' behind,
An' hunger fer 'em somehow, with 'em allus on yer mind.
It don't make any differunce how rich ye get t' be,
How much yer chairs an' tables cost, how great yer luxury;
It ain't home t' ye, though it be the palace of a king,
Until somehow yer soul is sort o' wrapped round
    everything.

Home ain't a place that gold can buy or get up in a minute;
Afore it's home there's got t' be a heap o' livin' in it;
Within the walls there's got t' be some babies born, and then
Right there ye've got t' bring 'em up t' women good, an'
    men;
And gradjerly, as time goes on, ye find ye wouldn't part
With anything they ever used—they've grown into yer
    heart:
The old high chairs, the playthings, too, the little shoes they
    wore

Ye hoard; an' if ye could ye'd keep the thumb marks on the
    door.

Ye've got t' weep t' make it home, ye've got t' sit an' sigh
An' watch beside a loved one's bed, an' know that Death is
    nigh;
An' in the stillness o' the night t' see Death's angel come,
An' close the eyes o' her that smiled,
    an' leave her sweet voice dumb.
Fer these are scenes that grip the heart,
    an' when yer tears are dried,
Ye find the home is dearer than it was, an' sanctified;
An' tuggin' at ye always are the pleasant memories
O' her that was an' is no more—ye can't escape from these.

Ye've got t' sing an' dance fer years, ye've got t' romp an' play,
An' learn t' love the things ye have by usin' 'em each day;
Even the roses 'round the porch must blossom year by year
Afore they 'come a part o' ye, suggestin' someone dear
Who used t' love 'em long ago, an' trained 'em jes' t' run
The way they do, so's they would get the early mornin' sun;
Ye've got t' love each brick an' stone from cellar up t' dome:
It takes a heap o' livin' in a house t' make it home.

TAKE HOME A SMILE

Edgar Guest
(1881–1959)

Take home a smile; forget the petty cares,
The dull, grim grind of all the day's affairs;
The day is done, come be yourself awhile:
To-night, to those who wait, take home a smile.

Take home a smile; don't scatter grief and gloom
Where laughter and light hearts should always bloom;
What though you've traveled many a dusty mile,
Footsore and weary, still take home a smile.

Take home a smile—it is not much to do,
But much it means to them who wait for you;
You can be brave for such a little while;
The day of doubt is done—take home a smile.

Known today mostly for his adventure novels (and of course for creating Dr. Jekyll and Mr. Hyde), Stevenson was a pioneering writer of children's poetry as well. A Child's Garden of Verses, first published in 1885, created a special world apart for children, in which they could let their imagination wander where it might, something that often has a great deal of appeal for adults as well.

BLOCK CITY

Robert Louis Stevenson
(1850-1894)

What are you able to build with your blocks?
Castles and palaces, temples and docks.
Rain may keep raining, and others go roam,
But I can be happy and building at home.

Let the sofa be mountains, the carpet be sea,
There I'll establish a city for me:
A kirk and a mill and a palace beside,
And a harbor as well where my vessels may ride.

Great is the palace with pillar and wall,
A sort of a tower on top of it all,
And steps coming down in an orderly way
To where my toy vessels lie safe in the bay.

This one is sailing and that one is moored:
Hark to the song of the sailors on board!
And see on the steps of my palace, the kings
Coming and going with presents and things!

The elder Oliver Wendell Holmes, father of the celebrated Supreme Court justice, was one of the founders of the New England school of thought called Transcendentalism. This poem is perhaps the most eloquent poetic expression of this philosophy, that nature is both a reflection of and a model for human existence and aspiration. The nautilus is a mollusk whose shell forms a winding spiral of chambers. Two humorous poems by Holmes appear on pp. 50 and 55.

THE CHAMBERED NAUTILUS

Oliver Wendell Holmes
(1809-1894)

This is the ship of pearl, which, poets feign,
Sails the unshadowed main,
The venturous bark that flings
On the sweet summer wind its purpled wings
In gulfs enchanted, where the Siren sings,
And coral reefs lie bare,
Where the cold sea-maids rise to sun their streaming hair.

Its webs of living gauze no more unfurl;
Wrecked is the ship of pearl!
And every chambered cell,
Where its dim dreaming life was wont to dwell,
As the frail tenant shaped his growing shell,
Before thee lies revealed,
Its irised ceiling rent, its sunless crypt unsealed!

Year after year beheld the silent toil
That spread his lustrous coil;
Still, as the spiral grew,
He left the past year's dwelling for the new,
Stole with soft steps its shining archway through,
Built up its idle door,
Stretched in his last-found home, and knew the old no more.

Thanks for the heavenly message brought by thee,
Child of the wandering sea,
Cast from her lap, forlorn!
From thy dead lips a clearer note is born
Than ever Triton blew from wreathèd horn!
While on mine ear it rings,
Through the deep caves of thought I hear a voice that sings:

Build thee more stately mansions, O my soul,
As the swift seasons roll!
Leave thy low-vaulted past!
Let each new temple, nobler than the last,
Shut thee from heaven with a dome more vast,
Till thou at length art free,
Leaving thine outgrown shell by life's unresting sea!

In our darkest hours, it might seem that there is little to celebrate. Yet Rudyard Kipling believed that we live through some of our most inspiring moments when all seems lost. Whether it's having the patience to wait for one true friend or searching inside oneself for the strength to carry on, the following poems suggest that up-lifting and beautiful experiences can be born out of hardship.

THE THOUSANDTH MAN

Rudyard Kipling

(1865–1936)

One man in a thousand, Solomon says,
Will stick more close than a brother.
And it's worth while seeking him half your days
If you find him before the other.
Nine hundred and ninety-nine depend
On what the world sees in you,
But the Thousandth Man will stand your friend
With the whole round world agin you.

'Tis neither promise nor prayer nor show
Will settle the finding for 'ee.
Nine hundred and ninety-nine of 'em go
By your looks, or your acts, or your glory.
But if he finds you and you find him,
The rest of the world don't matter;
For the Thousandth Man will sink or swim
With you in any water.

You can use his purse with no more talk
Than he uses yours for his spendings,
And laugh and meet in your daily walk
As though there had been no lendings.
Nine hundred and ninety-nine of 'em call
For silver and gold in their dealings;
But the Thousandth Man he's worth 'em all,
Because you can show him your feelings.

His wrong's your wrong, and his right's your right,
In season or out of season.
Stand up and back it in all men's sight—
With that for your only reason!
Nine hundred and ninety-nine can't bide
The shame or mocking or laughter,
But the Thousandth Man will stand by your side
To the gallows-foot—and after!

IF

Rudyard Kipling
(1865–1936)

If you can keep your head when all about you
Are losing theirs and blaming it on you,
If you can trust yourself when all men doubt you
But make allowance for their doubting too,
If you can wait and not be tired by waiting,
Or being lied about, don't deal in lies,
Or being hated, don't give way to hating,
And yet don't look too good, nor talk too wise:

If you can dream—and not make dreams your master,
If you can think—and not make thoughts your aim;
If you can meet with Triumph and Disaster
And treat those two impostors just the same;
If you can bear to hear the truth you've spoken
Twisted by knaves to make a trap for fools,
Or watch the things you gave your life to, broken,
And stoop and build 'em up with worn-out tools:

If you can make one heap of all your winnings
And risk it all on one turn of pitch-and-toss,
And lose, and start again at your beginnings
And never breathe a word about your loss;
If you can force your heart and nerve and sinew
To serve your turn long after they are gone,
And so hold on when there is nothing in you
Except the Will which says to them: "Hold on!"

If you can talk with crowds and keep your virtue,
Or walk with kings—nor lose the common touch,
If neither foes nor loving friends can hurt you;
If all men count with you, but none too much,
If you can fill the unforgiving minute
With sixty seconds' worth of distance run,
Yours is the Earth and everything that's in it,
And—which is more—you'll be a Man, my son!

American lyricist Sheldon Harnick wrote this popular song in 1953. Though the lyrics are cynical, they are accompanied by a humorously upbeat tune. This satirical response to the political climate of the time could easily be applied to our world today.

MERRY LITTLE MINUET

Sheldon Harnick

(1924–)

There are days in my life
when everything is dreary.
I grow pessimistic,
sad and world weary.
But when I am tearful
and fearfully upset,
I always sing
this merry little minuet.

They're rioting in Africa.
They're starving in Spain.
There's hurricanes in Florida
and Texas needs rain.

The whole world is festering
with unhappy souls.
The French hate the Germans;
the Germans hate the Poles.
Italians hate Yugoslavs;

South Africans hate the Dutch
and I don't like anybody very much.

In faraway Siberia,
they freeze by the score.
An avalanche in Switzerland
just got fifteen more.

But we can be tranquil
and thankful and proud
for man's been endowed
with a mushroom shaped cloud.
And we know for certain
that some lucky day
someone will set the spark off
and we will all be blown away.

They're rioting in Africa.
There's strife in Iran.
What nature doesn't do to us
will be done by our fellow man.

Edna St. Vincent Millay's poems capture the youthful spirit of the Roaring Twenties. In the following poems, Millay portrays romantic people who savor the present and discover beauty in fleeting moments of rebellion.

RECUERDO

Edna St. Vincent Millay
(1892–1950)

We were very tired, we were very merry—
We had gone back and forth all night on the ferry.
It was bare and bright, and smelled like a stable—
But we looked into a fire, we leaned across a table,
We lay on a hill-top underneath the moon;
And the whistles kept blowing, and the dawn came soon.

We were very tired, we were very merry—
We had gone back and forth all night on the ferry;
And you ate an apple, and I ate a pear,
From a dozen of each we had bought somewhere;
And the sky went wan, and the wind came cold,
And the sun rose dripping, a bucketful of gold.

We were very tired, we were very merry,
We had gone back and forth all night on the ferry.
We hailed "Good morrow, mother!" to a shawl-covered head,
And bought a morning paper, which neither of us read;
And she wept, "God bless you!" for the apples and pears,
And we gave her all our money but our subway fares.

AFTERNOON ON A HILL

Edna St. Vincent Millay
(1892–1950)

I will be the gladdest thing
    Under the sun!
I will touch a hundred flowers
    And not pick one.

I will look at cliffs and clouds
    With quiet eyes,
Watch the wind bow down the grass,
    And the grass rise.

And when lights begin to show
    Up from the town,
I will mark which must be mine,
    And then start down!

Everyone feels out of place at one time or another, but Phyllis Mc-Ginley urges us to embrace our complexity in the following poem. McGinley suggests that human beings are inherently unique, and with each new stanza, being different becomes more appealing.

IN PRAISE OF DIVERSITY

Phyllis McGinley

(1905–1978)

Since the ingenious earth began
    To shape itself from fire and rubble;
Since God invented man, and man
    At once fell to, inventing trouble,
One virtue, one subversive grace
Has chiefly vexed the human race.

One whimsical beatitude,
    Concocted for his gain and glory,
Has man most stoutly misconstrued
    Of all the primal category—
Counting no blessing, but a flaw,
That *Difference* is the mortal law.

Adam, perhaps, while toiling late,
    With life a book still strange to read in,
Saw his new world, how variegate,
    And mourned, "It was not so in Eden,"
Confusing thus from the beginning
Unlikeness with original sinning.

And still the sons of Adam's clay
  Labor in person or by proxy
At altering to a common way
  The planet's holy heterodoxy.
Till now, so dogged is the breed,
Almost it seems that they succeed.

One shrill, monotonous, level note
  The human orchestra's reduced to.
Man casts his ballot, turns his coat,
  Gets born, gets buried as he used to,
Makes war, makes love—but with a kind
Of masked and universal mind.

His good has no nuances. He
  Doubts or believes with total passion.
Heretics choose for heresy
  Whatever's the prevailing fashion.
Those wearing Tolerance for a label
Call other views intolerable.

"For or Against" 's the only rule.
  Damned are the unconvinced, the floaters.
Now all must go to public school,
  March with the League of Women Voters,
Or else for safety get allied
With a unanimous Other Side.

There's white, there's black; no tint between.
  Truth is a plane that was a prism.
All's Blanshard that's not Bishop Sheen.
  All's treason that's not patriotism.

Faith, charity, hope—now all must fit
One pattern or its opposite.

Or so it seems. Yet who would dare
    Deny that nature planned it other,
When every freckled thrush can wear
    A dapple various from his brother,
When each pale snowflake in the storm
Is false to some imagined norm?

Recalling then what surely was
    The earliest bounty of Creation:
That not a blade among the grass
    But flaunts its difference with elation,
Let us devoutly take no blame
If similar does not mean the same.

And grateful for the wit to see
    Prospects through doors we cannot enter,
Ah! Let us praise Diversity
    Which holds the world upon its center.
Praise *con amor'* or *furioso*
The large, the little, and the soso.

Rejoice that under cloud and star
    The planet's more than Maine or Texas.
Bless the delighful fact there are
    Twelve months, nine muses, and two sexes;
And infinite in earth's dominions
Arts, climates, and opinions.

Praise ice and ember, sand and rock,
   Tiger and dove and ends and sources;
Space travelers, and who only walk
   Like mailmen round familiar courses;
Praise vintage grapes and tavern Grappas,
And bankers and Phi Beta Kappas;

Each in its moment justified,
   Praise knowledge, theory, second guesses;
That which must wither or abide;
   Prim men, and men like wildernesses;
And men of peace and men of mayhem
And pipers and the ones who pay 'em.

Praise the disheveled, praise the sleek;
   Austerity and hearts-and-flowers;
People who turn the other cheek
   And extroverts who take cold showers;
Saints we can name a holy day for
And infidels the saints can pray for.

Praise youth for pulling things apart,
   Toppling the idols, breaking leases;
Then from the upset apple-cart
   Praise oldsters picking up the pieces.
Praise wisdom, hard to be a friend to,
And folly one can condescend to.

Praise what conforms and what is odd,
   Remembering, if the weather worsens
Along the way, that even God
   Is said to be three separate Persons.

Then upright or upon the knee
Praise Him that by His courtesy,
For all our prejudice and pains,
Diverse His Creature still remains.

Elizabeth Bishop discovered homes in new and exciting places during her travels across the globe. The filling station in the following poem could easily be found on any of the roads she traveled along, where she might have caught a glimpse of a charmingly untidy family united by their love for one another.

FILLING STATION

Elizabeth Bishop

(1911–1979)

Oh, but it is dirty!
—this little filling station,
oil-soaked, oil-permeated
to a disturbing, over-all
black translucency.
Be careful with that match!

Father wears a dirty,
oil-soaked monkey suit
that cuts him under the arms,
and several quick and saucy
and greasy sons assist him
(it's a family filling station),
all quite thoroughly dirty.

Do they live in the station?
It has a cement porch
behind the pumps, and on it
a set of crushed and grease-

impregnated wickerwork;
on the wicker sofa
a dirty dog, quite comfy.

Some comic books provide
the only note of color—
of certain color. They lie
upon a big dim doily
draping a taboret
(part of the set), beside
a big hirsute begonia.

Why the extraneous plant?
Why the taboret?
Why, oh why, the doily?
(Embroidered in daisy stitch
with marguerites, I think,
and heavy with gray crochet.)

Somebody embroidered the doily.
Somebody waters the plant,
or oils it, maybe. Somebody
arranges the rows of cans
so that they softly say:
ESSO—SO—SO—SO

to high-strung automobiles.
Somebody loves us all.

Pulitzer Prize winner Gwendolyn Brooks gleaned the inspiration for her urban poetry directly from the city streets. "The Rites for Cousin Vit" portrays the rebelliousness and vitality of people she encountered on the South Side of Chicago. The second poem has been widely but erroneously attributed to Brooks due to its striking similarity to her work. Like many of Brooks's poems, "Corners on the Curving Sky" indicates that individuality can link people together rather than separate them from one another.

THE RITES FOR COUSIN VIT

Gwendolyn Brooks
(1917–2000)

Carried her unprotesting out the door
Kicked back the casket-stand. But it can't hold her,
That stuff and satin aiming to enfold her,
The lid's contrition nor the bolts before.
Oh oh. Too much. Too much. Even now, surmise,
She rises in sunshine. There she goes
Back to the bars she knew and the repose
In love-rooms and the things in people's eyes.
Too vital and too squeaking. Must emerge.
Even now, she does the snake-hips with a hiss,
Slaps the bad wine across her shantung, talks
Of pregnancy, guitars and bridgework, walks
In parks or alleys, comes haply on the verge
Of happiness, haply hysterics. Is.

CORNERS ON THE CURVING SKY

Anonymous

Our earth is round, and, among other things
That means that you and I can hold
completely different
Points of view and both be right.
The difference of our positions will show
Stars in your window. I cannot even imagine.
Your sky may burn with light,
While mine, at the same moment,
·Spreads beautiful to darkness.
Still, we must choose how we separately corner
The circling universe of our experience
Once chosen, our cornering will determine
The message of any star and darkness we
encounter.

American actor and playwright John Howard Payne was probably unaware that this adaptation of a song from the opera Clari, Maid of Milan would become an instant sensation around the world. Payne was already an acclaimed actor living in England when he wrote the lyrics to "Home, Sweet Home," and perhaps he was dreaming of returning to American shores with each wistful line.

HOME, SWEET HOME

John Howard Payne
(1791–1852)

'Mid pleasures and palaces though we may roam,
Be it ever so humble there's no place like home!
A charm from the skies seems to hallow us there,
Which, seek through the world, is ne'er met with elsewhere.
Home! Home! Sweet, sweet home!
There's no place like home!
There's no place like home!

An exile from home splendor dazzles in vain;
Oh, give me my lowly thatch'd cottage again!
The birds singing gaily that came at my call;
Give me them with the peace of mind clearer than all.
Home! Home! Sweet, sweet home!
There's no place like home!
There's no place like home!

Robert Lowry wrote this hymn on a hot summer day, when the oppressive heat drew his mind to cool, refreshing water, and his daydream led to visions of people gathering by the river to celebrate life.

BEAUTIFUL RIVER

Robert Lowry
(1826–1899)

Shall we gather at the river
Where bright angel feet have trod;
With its crystal tide forever
Flowing by the throne of God?

Yes, we'll gather at the river,
The beautiful, the beautiful river—
Gather with the saints at the river
That flows by the throne of God.

On the margin of the river,
Washing up its silver spray,
We will walk and worship ever,
All the happy, golden day.

Yes, we'll gather at the river,
The beautiful, the beautiful river—
Gather with the saints at the river
That flows by the throne of God.

On the bosom of the river,
Where the Saviour-king we own,
We shall meet, and sorrow never
'Neath the glory of the throne.

Yes, we'll gather at the river,
The beautiful, the beautiful river—
Gather with the saints at the river
That flows by the throne of God.

Ere we reach the shining river,
Lay we every burden down;
Grace our spirits will deliver,
And provide a robe and crown.

Yes, we'll gather at the river,
The beautiful, the beautiful river—
Gather with the saints at the river
That flows by the throne of God.

At the smiling of the river,
Rippling with the Saviour's face,
Saints, whom death will never sever,
Lift their songs of saving grace.

Yes, we'll gather at the river,
The beautiful, the beautiful river—
Gather with the saints at the river
That flows by the throne of God.

Soon we'll reach the shining river,
Soon our pilgrimage will cease,

Soon our happy hearts will quiver
With the melody of peace.

Yes, we'll gather at the river,
The beautiful, the beautiful river—
Gather with the saints at the river
That flows by the throne of God.

This Appalachian folksong became an instant hit when it was per-
formed by the Carter Family in 1928, but it is most remembered
as a solo by June Carter Cash. June often had trouble hitting the
right notes when she sang, but rather than give up she decided
to use humor to stand out on the stage. With her ability to smile
through hardship, June epitomized the upbeat lyrics in this song.

KEEP ON THE SUNNY SIDE

Traditional

There's a dark and a troubled side of life.
There's a bright, there's a sunny side, too.
Tho' we meet with the darkness and strife
The sunny side we also may view.

Keep on the sunny side, always on the sunny side,
Keep on the sunny side of life.
It will help us ev'ry day, it will brighten all the way
If we'll keep on the sunny side of life.

The storm and its fury broke today,
Crushing hopes that we cherish so dear;
Clouds and storms will, in time, pass away.
The sun again will shine bright and clear.

Keep on the sunny side, always on the sunny side,
Keep on the sunny side of life.
It will help us ev'ry day, it will brighten all the way
If we'll keep on the sunny side of life.

Let us greet with the song of hope each day
Tho' the moment be cloudy or fair.
Let us trust in our Saviour away
Who keepeth everyone in His care.

Keep on the sunny side, always on the sunny side,
Keep on the sunny side of life.
It will help us ev'ry day, it will brighten all the way
If we'll keep on the sunny side of life.

ACKNOWLEDGMENTS

"The Adventures of Isabel" by Ogden Nash. Copyright © 1936 by Odgen Nash. Reprinted by permission of Curtis Brown, Ltd.

"Dawn Revisited", from ON THE BUS WITH ROSA PARKS by Rita Dove. Copyright © 1999 by Rita Dove. Used by permission of W. W. Norton & Company, Inc.

"Don't Worry, Be Happy" by Bobby McFerrin. Copyright © by Bobby McFerrin. Reprinted by permission of ProbNoblem Music.

"Filling Station" from THE COMPLETE POEMS 1927–1979 by Elizabeth Bishop. Copyright © 1979, 1983 by Alice Helen Methfessel. Reprinted by permission of Farrar, Straus and Giroux, LLC.

Excerpts from "Gus: The Theatre Cat" and "The Old Gumbie Cat" in OLD POSSUM'S BOOK OF PRACTICAL CATS, copyright 1939 by T.S. Eliot and renewed 1967 by Esme Valerie Eliot, reprinted by permission of Harcourt, Inc.

"In Praise of Diversity," from THE LOVE LETTERS OF PHYLLIS McGINLEY by Phyllis McGinley, copyright 1951, 1952, 1953, 1954 by Phyllis McGinley; renewed © 1979, 1980, 1981, 1982 by Phyllis Hayden Blake. Used by permission of Viking Penguin, a division of Penguin Group (USA) Inc.

"I Shall Paint My Nails Red." Carole Satyamurti, *Stitching the Dark: New & Selected Poems* (Bloodaxe Books, 2007).

"I Wandered Lonely as a Clod." © 1958 E.C. Publications, Inc. All Rights Reserved. Used with Permission.

"Melinda Mae" by Shel Silverstein. Copyright © 2004 by EVIL EYE MUSIC, INC. Reprinted with permission from the Estate of Shel Silverstein and HarperCollins Children's Books.

INDEX TO TITLES AND AUTHORS